bbq

bbq

MURDOCH BOOKS

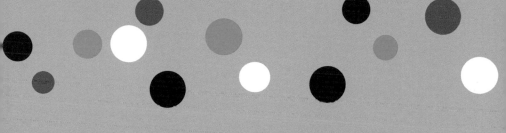

contents

fired up	7
beef	8
lamb	40
pork	68
chicken	96
seafood	126
vegetarian	170
index	196

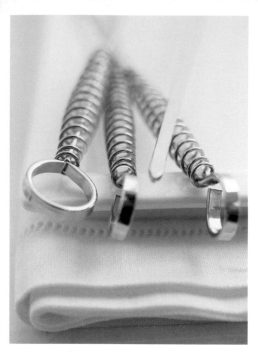

fired up

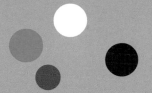

What's not to love about a barbecue? There's just something that the combination of smoke, flames and succulent chunks of charred, juicy meat has, that never fails to raise spirits. And spark appetites.

Ever since humans could kindle fire, we've been grilling things over it; initially out of bare necessity as there wasn't any other way to cook but these days we barbecue simply because we love the ritual involved and the sweet, earthy taste. That smoky sizzle, whether fired by coal, wood or gas, makes absolutely everything taste incredible, and eating barbecued foods is one of life's nicer social pleasures. Sausages and steak are standard 'barbie' fare and these meats are undeniably delicious. But there's so much more to barbecued food than 'snags', burgers and a few bits of sirloin. Fish, chicken and even vegetarian offerings can be barbecued.

Barbecuing suggests informality (after all, when else do you get to see a grown man in an apron?) but that's not to say a barbecue can't be posh. Toss some honey-roasted pork fillets or some salmon cutlets finished with sweet cucumber dressing on the barbecue menu and you've got a gourmet feast on your hands.

But the best thing about barbecuing is that it's all so easy. All you need for complete success are a few good ingredients, mastery of some simple techniques and well, this book. Oh and the barbecue, a little bit of outdoors space and a guy in an apron …

beef

Beef satay skewers

700 g (1 lb 9 oz) rump steak, cut into 2.5 cm (1 inch) cubes
2 small garlic cloves, crushed
3 teaspoons grated ginger
1 tablespoon fish sauce
2 small red chillies, seeded and julienned

Satay sauce
1 tablespoon peanut oil
8 red Asian shallots, finely chopped
8 garlic cloves, crushed

4 small red chillies, finely chopped
1 tablespoon finely chopped ginger
250 g (9 oz/1 cup) crunchy peanut butter
400 ml (14 fl oz) coconut milk
1 tablespoon soy sauce
60 g (2¼ oz/⅓ cup) grated palm sugar or soft brown sugar
3 tablespoons fish sauce
1 makrut (kaffir lime) leaf
4 tablespoons lime juice

Combine the steak with the garlic, ginger and fish sauce. Marinate, covered, in the refrigerator for at least 3 hours. Soak eight wooden skewers in cold water for 1 hour.

To make the satay sauce, heat the peanut oil in a saucepan over medium heat. Cook the shallots, garlic, chilli and ginger, stirring occasionally, for 5 minutes, or until the shallots are golden. Reduce the heat to low and add the peanut butter, coconut milk, soy sauce, palm sugar, fish sauce, makrut leaf and lime juice. Simmer for 10 minutes, or until thickened, then remove the leaf.

Thread the beef onto the skewers and cook on a barbecue grill plate over high heat for 6–8 minutes, or until cooked through, turning halfway through the cooking time. Top with the satay sauce and garnish with the julienned chilli. Serve with rice, if desired.

SERVES 4

Steak sandwich with balsamic onions

2 red onions	400 g (14 oz) piece of fillet
2 tablespoons olive oil	steak, cut into 1 cm (½ inch)
2 tablespoons balsamic vinegar	thick slices
1 tablespoon soft brown sugar	55 g (1¾ oz) baby rocket
8 large slices of sourdough	(arugula) leaves, rinsed and
bread	well drained

Preheat a barbecue flat plate to medium–high direct heat. Thinly slice the onions, separate the rings and toss with 1 tablespoon of olive oil.

Spread the onion across the flat plate and cook it for 10 minutes, or until softened and starting to brown. Pour the combined balsamic vinegar and sugar over them. Turn the onion so that it is well coated in the balsamic mixture, then spread it out a little and cook for a few more minutes, or until slightly glazed. Remove the onion from the barbecue.

Toast the bread on a barbecue grill plate for 30 seconds on each side, or until grill marks appear.

Brush the steaks with a little olive oil and season. Chargrill for 1 minute each side for medium–rare, or 2 minutes for well done.

To serve, put a piece of steak on a slice of toasted bread and top with the onion. Finish with a second piece of toast.

SERVES 4

Beef kebabs with mint yoghurt dressing

1 kg (2 lb 4 oz) lean beef fillet, cubed
125 ml (4 fl oz/½ cup) olive oil
4 tablespoons lemon juice
1 tablespoon chopped rosemary
2 small red onions, cut into wedges
200 g (7 oz) slender eggplants (aubergines), sliced

Mint yoghurt dressing
250 g (9 oz/1 cup) plain yoghurt
1 garlic clove, crushed
1 small Lebanese (short) cucumber, grated
2 tablespoons chopped mint

Put the beef in a non-metallic bowl. Combine the olive oil, lemon juice and rosemary and pour over the beef. Cover and refrigerate for 2 hours.

To make the mint yoghurt dressing, mix together the yoghurt, garlic, cucumber and mint and season.

Drain the beef and thread onto long metallic skewers, alternating pieces of beef with the onion wedges and slices of eggplant.

Cook the kebabs on a hot, lightly oiled barbecue grill or flat plate, turning often, for 5–10 minutes, or until the beef is cooked through and tender. Serve with the dressing.

MAKES 8 KEBABS

Beef and mozzarella burgers with tomatoes

500 g (1 lb 2 oz) minced
  (ground) beef
160 g (5¾ oz/2 cups) fresh
  breadcrumbs
1 red onion, finely chopped
4 garlic cloves, crushed
30 g (1 oz) finely shredded basil
  leaves
50 g (1¾ oz) pitted black olives,
  finely chopped

1 tablespoon balsamic vinegar
1 egg
8 pieces mozzarella cheese,
  2 cm x 3 cm x 5 mm (¾ x
  1¼ x ¼ inch)
olive oil spray

Chargrilled tomatoes
6 roma (plum) tomatoes
1½ tablespoons olive oil

Put the beef, breadcrumbs, onion, garlic, basil, olives, balsamic vinegar and egg in a large bowl and season. Use your hands to mix it all together, then cover and refrigerate the mixture for about 2 hours.

Divide the beef mixture into eight portions and roll each portion into a ball. Push a piece of mozzarella into the middle of each ball, then push the mince mixture over to cover the hole and flatten the ball to form a patty.

To make the chargrilled tomatoes, slice the tomatoes in half lengthways and toss them with the olive oil. Spray the barbecue grill plate with olive oil and preheat it to high direct heat. Cook the tomatoes, cut side down, for 8 minutes then turn them over and cook for another 5 minutes or until they are soft.

Cook the patties on one side for 5 minutes ,then flip and cook for a further 5 minutes or until they are completely cooked through and the cheese has melted. Serve the burgers and chargrilled tomatoes with a green salad.

SERVES 4

Cheeseburger with capsicum salsa

1 kg (2 lb 4 oz) minced (ground) beef
1 small onion, finely chopped
2 tablespoons chopped flat-leaf (Italian) parsley
1 teaspoon dried oregano
1 tablespoon tomato paste (concentrated purée)
70 g (2½ oz) cheddar cheese

6 bread rolls
salad leaves, to serve

Capsicum salsa
2 red capsicums (peppers)
1 tomato, finely chopped
1 small red onion, finely chopped
1 tablespoon olive oil
2 teaspoons red wine vinegar

Mix together the ground beef, onion, herbs and tomato paste and season well. Divide into six portions and shape into six patties. Cut the cheese into small squares. Make a cavity in the top of each patty with your thumb. Place a piece of cheese in the cavity and smooth the mince over to enclose the cheese completely.

To make the salsa, quarter the capsicums, remove the seeds and membranes and cook on a hot, lightly oiled barbecue grill, skin-side-down, until the skin blackens and blisters. Place in a plastic bag and leave to cool. Peel away the skin and dice the flesh. Combine with the tomato, onion, olive oil and vinegar and leave for at least 1 hour to let the flavours develop. Serve at room temperature.

Cook the patties on a hot, lightly oiled barbecue grill or flat plate for 4–5 minutes on each side, turning once. Serve in rolls with salad leaves and capsicum salsa.

SERVES 6

Thai beef skewers with peanut sauce

1 onion, chopped
2 garlic cloves, crushed
2 teaspoons sambal oelek
1 lemon grass stem, white part
only, chopped
2 teaspoons chopped fresh
ginger
1½ tablespoons oil
270 ml (9½ fl oz) coconut cream
125 g (4½ oz/½ cup) crunchy
peanut butter
1½ tablespoons fish sauce
2 teaspoons soy sauce

1 tablespoon grated palm sugar
or soft brown sugar
2 tablespoons lime juice
2 tablespoons chopped
coriander leaves
750 g (1 lb 10 oz) round or
rump steak, cut into 2 x
10 cm (¾ x 4 inch) pieces
2 teaspoons oil, extra
fresh red chilli, chopped,
to garnish (optional)
chopped roasted peanuts,
to garnish (optional)

Put the onion, garlic, sambal oelek, lemon grass and ginger in a food processor and process to a smooth paste.

Heat the oil in a saucepan over medium heat, add the paste and cook, stirring, for 2–3 minutes, or until fragrant. Add the coconut cream, peanut butter, fish sauce, soy sauce, sugar and lime juice and bring to the boil. Reduce the heat and simmer for 5 minutes, then stir in the coriander.

Meanwhile, thread the meat onto 12 metal skewers, and cook on a barbecue grill plate with the extra oil for 2 minutes each side, or until cooked to your liking. Garnish with chopped chilli and peanuts. Serve the skewers with rice and a salad on the side, if desired.

SERVES 4

Fillet steak with flavoured butters

4 fillet steaks

Capsicum butter
1 small red capsicum (pepper)
125 g (4½ oz) butter
2 teaspoons chopped oregano
2 teaspoons chopped chives

Garlic butter
125 g (4½ oz) butter
3 garlic cloves, crushed
2 spring onions (scallions), finely chopped

Cut a pocket in each steak.

For the capsicum butter, cut the capsicum into large pieces and place, skin-side up, under a hot grill (broiler) until the skin blisters and blackens. Put in a plastic bag until cool, then peel away the skin and dice the flesh.

Beat the butter until creamy. Add the capsicum, oregano and chives, season and beat until smooth.

To make the garlic butter, beat the butter until creamy, add the garlic and spring onion and beat until smooth.

Push capsicum butter into the pockets in two of the steaks and garlic butter into the other two. Cook on a hot, lightly oiled barbecue grill or flat plate for 4–5 minutes each side, brushing frequently with any remaining flavoured butter.

SERVES 4

Lemon and sage
veal chops with rocket

4 veal chops
2 tablespoons olive oil
1 tablespoon lemon juice
4 strips lemon zest
10 g (¼ oz) roughly chopped
    sage leaves
3 garlic cloves, peeled and
    bruised
lemon wedges, to serve

Rocket salad
100 g (3½ oz) rocket (arugula),
    washed and picked
1 avocado, sliced
1½ tablespoons extra virgin
    olive oil
2 teaspoons balsamic vinegar

Trim any fat and sinew from the chops and put in a shallow, non-metallic dish
with the olive oil, lemon juice, lemon zest, sage and garlic. Turn the chops to coat
evenly, then season. Cover and refrigerate for 4 hours or preferably overnight.

Put the rocket in a large serving bowl and scatter the avocado over it. Drizzle the
olive oil and balsamic vinegar over the salad, season and toss gently.

Preheat a barbecue grill plate to medium–high direct heat. Remove the chops from
the marinade, season well and grill for 5–6 minutes on each side, or until cooked
to your liking. Remove the chops from the barbecue, cover loosely with foil and
allow to rest for 5 minutes.

Serve the chops with the rocket salad and lemon wedges.

SERVES 4

Steak with balsamic onions

1½ tablespoons wholegrain
mustard
200 g (7 oz) crème fraîche
2 capsicums (peppers), 1 red
and 1 yellow, seeded and
quartered
2 zucchini (courgettes), trimmed
and sliced lengthways into
strips

2 tablespoons oil
2 large red onions, thinly sliced
4 rump steaks (about 200 g/7 oz
each)
2 tablespoons soft brown sugar
3 tablespoons balsamic vinegar

Preheat a barbecue grill plate to hot. Combine the mustard and crème fraîche in a bowl and season. Cover and set aside.

Brush the capsicum and zucchini with 1 tablespoon oil. Cook the capsicum, turning regularly, for 5 minutes, or until tender and slightly charred. Remove and cover with foil. Repeat with the zucchini, cooking for 5 minutes.

Heat the remaining oil on a flat plate, then cook the onion, turning occasionally, for 5–10 minutes, or until softened. Push to the side of the flat plate, then add the steaks and cook on each side for 3–4 minutes, or until cooked to your liking. Remove the steaks and cover with foil. Spread the onion over the flat plate, reduce the heat, sprinkle with sugar and cook for 1–2 minutes, or until the sugar has dissolved. Add the vinegar, stirring for 1–2 minutes, or until it is absorbed.

Peel the capsicum, then divide among serving plates with the zucchini. Place the steaks on top, season and top with the balsamic onions. Serve with the mustard crème fraîche.

SERVES 4

Sesame and ginger beef

3 tablespoons sesame oil
3 tablespoons soy sauce
2 garlic cloves, crushed
2 tablespoons grated fresh ginger
1 tablespoon lemon juice
2 tablespoons chopped spring onions (scallions)
60 g (2¼ oz/⅓ cup) soft brown sugar
500 g (1 lb 2 oz) beef fillet

Combine the sesame oil, soy sauce, garlic, ginger, lemon juice, spring onion and brown sugar in a non-metallic dish. Add the beef and coat well with the marinade. Cover and refrigerate for at least 2 hours, or overnight if possible.

Brown the beef on all sides on a very hot, lightly oiled barbecue grill or flat plate. When the beef is sealed, remove, wrap in foil and return to the barbecue, turning occasionally, for a further 15–20 minutes, depending on how well done you like your meat. Leave for 10 minutes before slicing.

Put the leftover marinade in a small saucepan and boil for 5 minutes. Serve as a sauce with the beef.

SERVES 4–6

Rosemary and red wine steaks with vegetables

12 small new potatoes
3 tablespoons olive oil
1 tablespoon finely chopped
    rosemary
6 garlic cloves, sliced
sea salt flakes, to season

4 large, thick field mushrooms
12 asparagus spears
250 ml (1 cup) red wine
4 scotch fillet steaks (about
    250 g/9 oz each)

Heat a barbecue grill plate to hot. Toss the new potatoes with 1 tablespoon of oil, half the rosemary and half the garlic and season with the sea salt. Divide the potatoes among four large sheets of foil and wrap up into neat packages, sealing firmly around the edges. Place on the barbecue and cook, turning frequently for 30–40 minutes, or until tender.

Meanwhile, brush the mushrooms and asparagus with a little oil and set aside.

Put the wine, remaining oil, rosemary and garlic in a non-metallic dish and season with pepper. Add the steaks and turn to coat well in the marinade. Leave for 25 minutes, then drain.

Put the steaks on the barbecue with the mushrooms and cook for 4 minutes each side, or until cooked to your liking. Transfer the steaks and mushrooms to a plate, cover lightly and allow to rest. Add the asparagus to the barbecue, turning regularly for about 2 minutes, or until tender. By this stage your potatoes should be cooked. Season. Serve the steaks with the mushrooms, asparagus spears and potatoes.

SERVES 4

Pepper steaks with horseradish sauce

4 sirloin steaks
3 tablespoons seasoned cracked pepper

Horseradish sauce
2 tablespoons brandy
3 tablespoons beef stock
4 tablespoons pouring (whipping) cream
1 tablespoon horseradish cream
1/2 teaspoon sugar

Coat the steaks on both sides with pepper, pressing it into the meat.

Cook on a hot, lightly oiled barbecue grill or flat plate for 5–10 minutes, until cooked to your liking.

To make the sauce, put the brandy and stock in a pan. Bring to the boil, then reduce the heat. Stir in the cream, horseradish and sugar and heat through. Serve with the steaks.

SERVES 4

Roast sirloin with mustard pepper crust

90 g (3¼ oz) Dijon mustard
2 tablespoons light soy sauce
2 tablespoons plain (all-purpose) flour
3 tablespoons olive oil
3 teaspoons chopped thyme leaves
4 garlic cloves, crushed
2.5 kg (5 lb 8 oz) piece of sirloin, trimmed

40 g (1½ oz) butter, melted
1 onion, roughly diced
1 large carrot, roughly diced
2 celery stalks, roughly chopped
250 ml (9 fl oz/1 cup) red wine
500 ml (17 fl oz/2 cups) beef stock
2 bay leaves
2 teaspoons cornflour (cornstarch)

Mix the mustard, soy sauce, flour, 2 tablespoons of oil, 2 teaspoons of thyme, two of the crushed garlic cloves and 1 tablespoon of cracked black pepper in a bowl.

Coat the sirloin with the mustard mixture, put it on a wire rack over a tray and refrigerate for 1 hour so the crust sets.

Heat the remaining olive oil in a saucepan. Add the onion, carrot, celery and remaining garlic and cook for 5 minutes. Pour in the red wine, cook for a further 5 minutes, then add the beef stock, the bay leaves and the remaining thyme. Mix the cornflour with 1 tablespoon water and add it to the pan. Simmer over low heat for 20 minutes, or until it is slightly thickened, then strain and season to taste.

Preheat a kettle or covered barbecue to medium indirect heat, put the sirloin in the middle of the barbecue. Replace the cover and cook for 45 minutes. Remove the sirloin from the barbecue, and leave to rest, covered, for about 10 minutes before carving. Serve with the red wine sauce and asparagus and potatoes, if desired.

SERVES 6–8

Veal steaks with caper butter

50 g (1¾ oz) butter, softened
2 tablespoons dry white wine
2 tablespoons capers, finely chopped
2 teaspoons finely grated lemon zest
8 small veal steaks, about 500 g (1 lb 2 oz)
mixed salad greens, to serve

Mix together the butter, white wine, capers, lemon zest and some salt and black pepper with a wooden spoon. Shape into a log, cover and refrigerate until required.

Cook the veal steaks on a hot, lightly oiled barbecue grill or flat plate for 2–3 minutes on each side. Remove, place on warm plates and top with slices of the caper butter. Serve immediately with salad greens.

SERVES 4

Roast beef with barbecue sauce

2 tablespoons paprika
1 tablespoon onion powder
1 tablespoon garlic powder
2 teaspoons sugar
1 teaspoon chilli powder
3 tablespoons oil
1.5 kg (3 lb 5 oz) piece beef fillet

Barbecue sauce
2 tablespoons oil
1 small onion, finely chopped

4 garlic cloves, crushed
½ teaspoon chilli flakes
1½ tablespoons paprika
375 ml (13 fl oz/1½ cups) tomato sauce (ketchup)
125 ml (4 fl oz/½ cup) beer
3 tablespoons cider vinegar
4 tablespoons soft brown sugar
2 tablespoons Dijon mustard
4 tablespoons Worcestershire sauce

Mix the paprika, onion powder, garlic powder, sugar, chilli powder, 2 teaspoons ground black pepper, 2 teaspoons salt and the oil in a small bowl. Rub the mixture all over the beef fillet, then cover with plastic wrap and refrigerate overnight.

To make the barbecue sauce, put the oil in a saucepan over medium heat, add the onion, garlic and chilli flakes, and cook for 5 minutes or until the onion is soft. Add the remaining ingredients and 3 tablespoons of water. Simmer over low heat for 20 minutes, or until slightly thickened. Season well and allow to cool.

Preheat a kettle or covered barbecue to medium indirect heat. Cook the beef, covered, for 40 minutes for rare or a further 10 minutes for medium.

Brush the sauce over the beef fillet and cook, covered, for a further 10 minutes. Remove from the barbecue, cover with foil and rest for 10 minutes. Carve and serve with the remaining barbecue sauce.

SERVES 6

lamb

Garlic and mint lamb skewers with yoghurt sauce

8 lamb fillets, trimmed and cut into 2.5 cm (1 inch) cubes
2 tablespoons olive oil
4 tablespoons lemon juice
2 garlic cloves, crushed
2 teaspoons dried mint leaves

Yoghurt sauce
250 g (9 oz/1 cup) Greek-style yoghurt
1 garlic clove, crushed

Put the lamb in a non-metallic bowl with the olive oil, lemon juice, garlic and mint. Mix until well combined and season with black pepper. Cover and refrigerate for at least 4 hours, or overnight. Soak eight wooden skewers in cold water for 1 hour.

To make the yoghurt sauce, mix the yoghurt and garlic in a small bowl. Refrigerate until you ready to use.

Thread the lamb onto the skewers and season well. Preheat the barbecue grill or flat plate to medium–high direct heat and cook the skewers for about 3–4 minutes on each side, or until cooked to your liking. Serve the skewers with the yoghurt sauce and couscous, if desired.

SERVES 4

Lamb kebabs

5 garlic cloves, roughly chopped
5 cm (2 inch) piece of ginger, roughly chopped
3 green chillies, roughly chopped
1 onion, roughly chopped
3 tablespoons Greek-style yoghurt
1 small handful coriander (cilantro) leaves
½ teaspoon ground black pepper
500 g (1 lb 2 oz) minced (ground) lamb
red onion rings, to garnish
lemon wedges, to serve

Combine the garlic, ginger, chilli, onion, yoghurt and coriander leaves in a food processor to form a thick smooth paste. Add the pepper, season with salt, then mix in the lamb.

Divide the meat into 16 portions, about 2 tablespoons each. Shape each portion into an oval patty, cover and refrigerate for 20 minutes.

Heat the barbecue grill plate to high. Using four metal skewers, thread four meatballs onto each. Cook for 7 minutes, or until browned. Turn over and cook on the other side. Serve with onion rings and lemon wedges.

SERVES 4

Herbed lamb burgers

750 g (1 lb 10 oz) minced (ground) lamb
2 tablespoons chopped basil
1 tablespoon chopped chives
1 tablespoon chopped rosemary
1 tablespoon chopped thyme
2 tablespoons lemon juice
80 g (2¾ oz/1 cup) fresh breadcrumbs
1 egg
2 long crusty bread sticks
lettuce leaves, rinsed and dried
2 tomatoes, sliced
tomato sauce (ketchup), to serve

Combine the lamb with the herbs, juice, breadcrumbs, egg and season.
Mix well. Divide the mixture into eight portions and shape into thick patties.

Put the burgers on a hot, lightly oiled barbecue grill or flat plate. Cook for
5–10 minutes each side until well browned and just cooked through.

Cut the bread sticks in half and fill with the burgers, lettuce, tomato and
tomato sauce.

MAKES 8 BURGERS

Lamb kofta

1 red onion, finely chopped
25 g (1 oz) chopped flat-leaf (Italian) parsley
25 g (1 oz) chopped coriander (cilantro) leaves
15 g (½ oz) chopped mint
1 tablespoon paprika
1 tablespoon ground cumin
1½ teaspoons allspice
½ teaspoon ground ginger
½ teaspoon chilli flakes
1.2 kg (2 lb 11 oz) minced (ground) lamb
3 tablespoons soda water
pitta breads, baba ghanoush and tabouleh, to serve (optional)

Put the onion, parsley, coriander, mint, paprika, cumin, allspice, ginger and chilli in a food processor and blend until combined. Season with 2 teaspoons salt and some freshly ground black pepper, then add the lamb to the food processor and process. Add the soda water in a thin stream until the mixture forms a smooth paste, then cover and refrigerate for at least 2 hours, or preferably overnight. Soak four wooden skewers in cold water for 1 hour.

Divide the lamb mixture into 12 portions and mould each portion into a torpedo shape, using damp hands to stop the meat from sticking. Cover and refrigerate.

Preheat a barbecue flat plate to medium–high direct heat. Brush the kofta lightly with olive oil and cook, turning frequently, for 10–12 minutes, or until evenly browned and cooked through. Serve the kofta with pitta bread, baba ganoush and tabouleh, if desired.

SERVES 4

Lamb pide with garlic and chickpea purée

1 tablespoon lemon juice
1 teaspoon ground cumin
1 tablespoon olive oil
4 trimmed lamb fillets
1 garlic bulb
100 g (3½ oz/½ cup) tinned chickpeas, drained
2 teaspoons lemon juice, extra
1 tablespoon plain yoghurt
4 x 100 g (3½ oz) pieces Turkish bread
2 tomatoes, thinly sliced
rocket (arugula) leaves, to serve

Mix the lemon juice, cumin, olive oil and season. Add the lamb fillets and leave to marinate for at least 1 hour.

Preheat the oven to 210°C (415°F/Gas 6–7). Wrap the bulb of garlic in foil, then roast for 20 minutes, or until soft. Cool, then squeeze out the pulp from each clove. Purée the pulp with the chickpeas, extra lemon juice and yoghurt in a food processor. Season.

Preheat a barbecue flat plate to medium–high direct heat. Cook the lamb for 3 minutes on each side, or until done to your liking. Grill (broil) or toast the bread, then slice through the middle and spread with the chickpea spread. Top with thin slices of the lamb, the tomato and some rocket leaves.

SERVES 4

Paprika lamb kebabs with skordalia

1 kg (2 lb 4 oz) lamb backstraps
  or eye of loin fillets, cut into
  2 cm (¾ inch) cubes
1 tablespoon sweet paprika
1 tablespoon hot paprika
125 ml (4 fl oz/½ cup) lemon
  juice

125 ml (4 fl oz/½ cup) olive oil
3 floury potatoes, cut into cubes
3–4 garlic cloves, crushed with a
  pinch of salt

Soak 12 wooden skewers in water for 30 minutes. Thread six lamb cubes onto each, then place in a non-metallic rectangular dish large enough to hold all the skewers in one layer.

Combine the paprikas, 4 tablespoons of lemon juice and 3 tablespoons of oil in a small non-metallic bowl. Pour over the skewers. Season. Cover and refrigerate.

To make the skordalia, boil the potatoes for 20 minutes, or until tender. Drain and put in a food processor with the garlic and 1 tablespoon of the lemon juice. With the motor running, slowly add the remaining oil in a thin stream and continue blending for 30–60 seconds, or until all the oil is incorporated. Season. Set aside to serve at room temperature.

Heat a barbecue grill plate and brush with oil. Cook the skewers for 3–4 minutes each side for medium–rare, or 5–6 minutes for well done.

Serve the kebabs with skordalia and spinach and lemon wedges, if desired.

SERVES 4

Lamb burger

1 tablespoon olive oil
1 onion, finely chopped
2 garlic cloves, crushed
1½ teaspoons ground cumin
800 g (1 lb 12 oz) minced
    (ground) lamb
2 tablespoons finely chopped
    flat-leaf (Italian) parsley
2 tablespoons finely chopped
    coriander (cilantro) leaves

2 red capsicums (peppers),
    quartered and seeded
1 tablespoon olive oil, extra
2 red onions, thinly sliced
olive oil spray
1 loaf Turkish bread, cut into
    4 pieces and split
100 g (3½ oz) baby rocket
    (arugula) leaves

Heat the oil in a frying pan and cook the onion over medium heat for 2–3 minutes or until softened. Add the garlic and cumin, cook it for another minute, then allow the mixture to cool. Put the onion mixture in a large bowl and add the lamb, parsley and coriander. Season and mix to combine. Divide the mixture into four portions, and shape each portion into a 2 cm (¾ inch) thick patty.

Heat the barbecue to medium–high direct heat. Toss the capsicum with the extra oil and cook it on the flat plate for 6 minutes on each side, or until lightly charred. Grill the patties on the flat plate for 5–6 minutes each side, or until they are done.

Spray the red onion with the olive oil spray and cook on the flat plate for 2–3 minutes, or until soft and golden. Toast the bread, cut-side down, on the grill plate for 1–2 minutes or until it is marked and golden.

To assemble the burgers, put some rocket on four of the bread slices. Put a patty on top, then the capsicum and onion. Season and top with the remaining bread slices and serve immediately.

SERVES 4

Lamb souvlaki roll

500 g (1 lb 2 oz) lamb backstrap or loin fillet
100 ml (3½ fl oz) olive oil
3 tablespoons dry white wine
1 tablespoon chopped oregano
3 tablespoons roughly chopped basil
3 garlic cloves, crushed
2 bay leaves, crushed
2½ tablespoons lemon juice
1 large loaf Turkish bread
250 g (9 oz/1 cup) baba ghanoush
1 tablespoon roughly chopped flat-leaf (Italian) parsley

Place the lamb fillet in a shallow non-metallic dish. Mix together the oil, wine, oregano, basil, garlic, bay leaves and 2 tablespoons of the lemon juice and pour over the lamb, turning to coat well. Cover with plastic wrap and marinate for 4 hours.

Cook the lamb on a hot, lightly oiled barbecue grill or flat plate for 6–8 minutes, or until seared but still pink in the centre. Remove from the heat and rest for 10 minutes, then cut into slices.

Split the Turkish bread lengthways and spread the bottom thickly with baba ghanoush. Top with the lamb slices, sprinkle with the parsley and remaining lemon juice, then season. Replace the top of the loaf, then cut into quarters to serve.

SERVES 4

Hoisin lamb with charred spring onion

800 g (1 lb 12 oz) lamb loin
3 tablespoons hoisin sauce
2 tablespoons soy sauce
2 garlic cloves, bruised
1 tablespoon grated fresh ginger
2 teaspoons olive oil
16 spring onions (scallions), trimmed to 18 cm (7 inches) long
40 g (1½ oz/¼ cup) chopped toasted peanuts

Trim the lamb of any excess fat and sinew. Combine the hoisin sauce, soy sauce, garlic, ginger and 1 teaspoon of the oil in a shallow dish, add the lamb and turn to coat well in the marinade. Cover the dish and refrigerate for 4 hours or overnight.

Toss the trimmed spring onions with the remaining oil and season well. Remove the lamb from the marinade, season the meat and pour the marinade into a small saucepan. Simmer the marinade for 5 minutes, or until it is slightly reduced. Preheat a barbecue grill plate to medium direct heat. Cook the lamb for 5–6 minutes on each side, or until it is cooked to your liking, brushing frequently with the marinade. Allow to rest, covered, for 3 minutes. Grill the spring onions for 1–2 minutes, or until they are tender, but still firm.

Cut the lamb across the grain into 2 cm (¾ inch) thick slices, and arrange on a serving plate. Drizzle any juices that have been released during resting over the lamb and sprinkle with the toasted peanuts. Serve with the spring onions.

SERVES 4

Lamb cutlets with mint gremolata

1 small handful mint leaves
1 tablespoon flat-leaf (Italian) parsley
2 garlic cloves
1½ tablespoons lemon zest (white pith removed),
    cut into thin strips
2 tablespoons extra virgin olive oil
8 French-trimmed lamb cutlets
2 carrots
2 zucchini (courgettes)
1 tablespoon lemon juice

To make the gremolata, finely chop the mint, parsley, garlic and lemon strips, then combine well.

Heat a barbecue grill plate to high heat. Lightly brush with 1 tablespoon of the oil. Cook the cutlets over medium heat for 2 minutes on each side, or until cooked to your liking. Remove the cutlets and cover to keep warm.

Trim the ends from the carrots and zucchini and, using a sharp vegetable peeler, peel the vegetables lengthways into ribbons. Heat the remaining oil in a large saucepan. Add the vegetables and toss over medium heat for 3–5 minutes, or until sautéed but tender.

Divide the cutlets among the serving plates, sprinkle the cutlets with the gremolata and drizzle with the lemon juice. Serve with the vegetable ribbons.

SERVES 4

Lamb chops with citrus pockets

4 lamb chump chops, about 250 g (9 oz) each
2 tablespoons lemon juice

Citrus filling
3 spring onions (scallions), finely chopped
1 celery stalk, finely chopped
2 teaspoons grated fresh ginger
60 g (2¼ oz/¾ cup) fresh breadcrumbs
2 tablespoons orange juice
2 teaspoons finely grated orange zest
1 teaspoon chopped rosemary

Cut a deep, long pocket in the side of each lamb chop. Mix together the spring onion, celery, ginger, breadcrumbs, orange juice, zest and rosemary and spoon into the pockets in the lamb.

Cook on a hot, lightly oiled barbecue flat plate for 15 minutes, turning once, or until the lamb is cooked through but still pink in the centre. Drizzle with the lemon juice before serving.

SERVES 4

Marinated lamb

15 g (½ oz/½ cup) finely chopped flat-leaf (Italian) parsley
20 g (¾ oz/⅓ cup) finely chopped coriander (cilantro) leaves
4 garlic cloves, crushed
1 tablespoon paprika
1 teaspoon dried thyme
125 ml (4 fl oz/½ cup) olive oil
3 tablespoons lemon juice
2 teaspoons ground cumin
4 x 250 g (9 oz) lamb rumps or pieces of tenderloin, trimmed

Mix the parsley, coriander, garlic, paprika, thyme, oil, lemon juice and 1½ teaspoons cumin together in a non-metallic dish. Score diagonal lines in the fat on the lamb pieces with a sharp knife, then put in the marinade, turning to coat evenly. Cover and refrigerate for at least 2 hours or overnight.

Heat a barbecue flat plate to medium direct heat. Season the lamb to taste with white pepper, the remaining ½ teaspoon of cumin and some salt. Cook the lamb fat-side up for 3 minutes and then cook the other side for 2–3 minutes, making sure the fat is well cooked. Remove from the barbecue as soon as it is done, cover with foil and set aside to rest for about 5 minutes before carving.

SERVES 4

Roast lamb

2.5 kg (5 lb 8 oz) leg of lamb
6 garlic cloves, peeled
2 tablespoons rosemary leaves
1 tablespoon olive oil

Make 12 small incisions in the fleshy parts of the lamb. Cut the garlic cloves in half lengthways, and push into the incisions with the rosemary leaves. Rub the lamb with the oil and season well.

Preheat a kettle or covered barbecue to medium indirect heat, put the lamb in the middle of the barbecue, replace the lid, and roast for 1 hour 30 minutes.

When the lamb is ready, remove from the barbecue and allow to rest, covered, for 10 minutes before carving. Serve with any juices that have been released while resting.

SERVES 6

pork

Pork skewers in green ginger wine and soy

800 g (1 lb 12 oz) pork fillets, trimmed
1 tablespoon finely grated fresh ginger
2 garlic cloves, finely chopped
1 tablespoon finely chopped preserved ginger in syrup
3 tablespoons green ginger wine (see Note)

2½ tablespoons kecap manis
½ teaspoon sesame oil
1 tablespoon oil
8 bulb spring onions (scallions), green parts removed, quartered
1 tablespoon olive oil
coriander (cilantro) sprigs, to garnish

Cut the pork into 12 x 2.5 cm (5 x 1 inch) strips and put in a non-metallic bowl with the ginger, garlic, preserved ginger, green ginger wine, kecap manis and oils. Cover and refrigerate. Leave to marinate for at least 2 hours, or overnight.

Soak 12 wooden skewers in cold water for 1 hour, then thread four pork strips into an S-shape onto each skewer. Cover the skewers and refrigerate until needed.

Preheat the barbecue to medium direct heat. Toss the spring onions with the olive oil and season. Cook on the flat plate for 10 minutes, or until softened and well browned. When the spring onions are nearly cooked, put the kebabs on the grill plate and grill for 2 minutes on each side, or until the pork is just cooked through and glazed. Garnish the skewers with coriander sprigs and serve immediately with the spring onion.

SERVES 4

NOTE: Green ginger wine is a sweet, fortified wine with a distinctive ginger flavour which originated in Britain.

Chinese-style
barbecue spareribs

3 tablespoons hoisin sauce
4 tablespoons oyster sauce
2 tablespoons rice wine
125 ml (4 fl oz/½ cup) soy sauce
6 garlic cloves, crushed
3 teaspoons finely grated fresh ginger
2 kg (4 lb 8 oz) American-style pork ribs
2 tablespoons honey

Mix the hoisin sauce, oyster sauce, rice wine, soy sauce, garlic and ginger in a large non-metallic bowl. Add the ribs and turn them so that they are coated in the marinade. Cover the bowl and refrigerate for at least 4 hours, or overnight.

Remove the ribs from the marinade and tip the marinade into a small saucepan with the honey. Simmer the mixture over low heat for 5 minutes, or until it becomes slightly syrupy—you will be using this to baste the ribs as they cook.

Heat a kettle or covered barbecue to medium indirect heat and cook the ribs, covered, for 10 minutes, then turn over and cook for a further 5 minutes. Continue cooking, basting and turning the ribs frequently for 30 minutes, or until cooked through and caramelized.

Once the ribs are cooked, allow to rest, covered, for 10 minutes, then cut the racks into individual ribs to serve.

SERVES 6

Spice-rubbed pork kebabs with garlic sauce

800 g (1 lb 12 oz) pork neck
fillet, trimmed
2 teaspoons fennel seeds
2 teaspoons coriander seeds
1 tablespoon olive oil

Garlic sauce
4 garlic cloves, coarsely chopped

1 thick slice of white bread,
crusts removed
3 tablespoons olive oil
1½ tablespoons lemon juice

lemon wedges
pitta bread

Soak eight wooden skewers in cold water for 1 hour. Cut the pork into 2 cm
(¾ inch) cubes.

Dry-fry the fennel and coriander seeds for about 30 seconds, or until fragrant, then
grind in a mortar and pestle. Mix the ground spices with the olive oil and mix with
the pork until well coated. Cover and refrigerate for 2 hours.

To make the garlic sauce, crush the garlic cloves in a mortar and pestle with
½ teaspoon salt until smooth. Tear the white bread into pieces and put in a bowl
with enough warm water to cover it. Allow to soak for 5 minutes, then squeeze
out the bread and add to the garlic, a little at a time, and pound until you have a
smooth paste. Add the olive oil, 1 tablespoon at a time. Add 3 tablespoons of
boiling water, one tablespoon at a time, and stir in the lemon juice.

Thread the pork onto the skewers and season well. Preheat the barbecue grill plate
to medium–high direct heat and cook the kebabs for 10 minutes, or until cooked
through, turning halfway through cooking. Serve with the garlic sauce and lemon
wedges and warm pitta bread, if desired.

SERVES 4

Pork sausage burgers
with mustard cream

800 g (1 lb 12 oz) minced (ground) pork
1 small onion, finely chopped
80 g (2¾ oz/1 cup) fresh breadcrumbs
2 garlic cloves, crushed
1 egg, lightly beaten
1 teaspoon dried sage
6 long bread rolls

Mustard cream
125 g (4½ oz/½ cup) sour cream
1 tablespoon wholegrain mustard
2 teaspoons lemon juice

Mix together the pork, onion, breadcrumbs, garlic, egg and sage. Season well.
Divide the mixture into six portions and shape into sausages.

Cook the sausages on a hot, lightly oiled barbecue flat plate for 5–10 minutes,
turning occasionally.

To make the mustard cream, put the sour cream, mustard and juice in a small
bowl and stir together. Spread each cut side of the rolls with a little mustard
cream, then sandwich the sausage burgers in the middle. Serve with the remaining
mustard cream.

SERVES 6

Sweet and sour pork kebabs

1 kg (2 lb 4 oz) pork fillets, cubed
1 large red capsicum (pepper), cubed
1 large green capsicum (pepper), cubed
425 g (15 oz) tinned pineapple pieces, drained, juice reserved
250 ml (9 fl oz/1 cup) orange juice
3 tablespoons white vinegar
2 tablespoons soft brown sugar
2 teaspoons chilli garlic sauce
2 teaspoons cornflour (cornstarch)

Soak 12 wooden skewers in water for 30 minutes. Thread the pork alternately with pieces of capsicum and pineapple onto the skewers.

Mix the pineapple juice with the orange juice, vinegar, sugar and sauce. Put the kebabs in a shallow non-metallic dish and pour over half the marinade. Cover and refrigerate for at least 3 hours, turning occasionally.

Put the remaining marinade in a small saucepan. Mix the cornflour with 1 tablespoon of the marinade until smooth, then add to the pan. Stir over medium heat until the mixture boils and thickens. Transfer to a bowl, cover the surface with plastic wrap and leave to cool.

Cook the kebabs on a hot, lightly oiled barbecue flat plate for 15 minutes, turning occasionally, until tender. Serve with the sauce.

SERVES 6

Chilli pork ribs

1 kg (2 lb 4 oz) pork spareribs
125 g (4½ oz) tinned puréed tomatoes
2 tablespoons honey
2 tablespoons chilli sauce
2 tablespoons hoisin sauce
2 tablespoons lime juice
2 garlic cloves, crushed
1 tablespoon oil

Cut each rib into thirds, then place in a single layer in a shallow non-metallic dish.

Combine all the remaining ingredients except the oil and pour over the meat, turning to coat well. Cover with plastic wrap and refrigerate overnight.

Drain the ribs, reserving the marinade. Cook over medium heat on a lightly oiled barbecue grill or flat plate. Baste often with the marinade and cook for 15–20 minutes, or until the ribs are tender and well browned, turning occasionally. Season to taste and serve immediately.

SERVES 4–6

Fennel and pork
sausages with onion relish

750 g (1 lb 10 oz) minced (ground) pork
40 g (1½ oz/½ cup) fresh breadcrumbs
2 garlic cloves, crushed
3 teaspoons fennel seeds, coarsely crushed
1 teaspoon finely grated orange zest
2 teaspoons chopped thyme leaves
1 small handful flat-leaf (Italian) parsley, chopped

oil, for brushing
4 long, crusty rolls
50 g (1¾ oz) butter, softened
60 g (2¼ oz) rocket (arugula) leaves
1 tablespoon olive oil
1 teaspoon balsamic vinegar

Onion relish
50 g (1¾ oz) butter
2 red onions, thinly sliced
1 tablespoon soft brown sugar
2 tablespoons balsamic vinegar

Put the pork, breadcrumbs, garlic, fennel seeds, zest, thyme and parsley in a bowl. Season well and mix to combine. Cover and refrigerate for 4 hours, or overnight.

To make the onion relish, melt the butter in a heavy-based saucepan. Add the onion and cook, stirring, over low heat for about 10 minutes, or until softened. Add the sugar and vinegar, and continue to cook for a further 30 minutes.

Preheat a barbecue flat plate to medium direct heat. Divide the pork mixture into eight portions and mould each portion into a flattish sausage shape. Brush the sausages with oil and cook for 8 minutes on each side, or until cooked through.

To assemble, split the rolls down the middle and butter them. Toss the rocket with the olive oil and balsamic vinegar, and put some of the leaves in each of the rolls. Top with a sausage and some of the onion relish.

MAKES 8

Pork loin with apple glaze and wedges

1 teaspoon aniseed
135 g (4¾ oz/½ cup) apple sauce
2 tablespoons soft brown sugar
1.5 kg (3 lb 5 oz) boned pork loin with the skin on
2 teaspoons oil
4 large potatoes, each cut into 8 wedges
2 tablespoons olive oil
2 teaspoons garlic salt

Dry-fry the aniseed over medium heat for 30 seconds, or until fragrant. Add the apple sauce and sugar, reduce the heat to low and cook, stirring, for 1 minute.

Use a sharp knife to remove the skin from the pork loin. Score the skin in a diamond pattern and rub the oil and 1 tablespoon salt over the skin, working into the cuts. Put the potato wedges in a bowl with the olive oil and garlic salt, season with black pepper and toss until well coated.

Preheat a kettle or covered barbecue to medium indirect heat. Tie the pork loin with string to help keep its shape, then put the pork and the skin in the barbecue and arrange the wedges around them. After 30 minutes, baste the pork with the apple glaze, and repeat every 10 minutes for a further 30 minutes. Turn the skin and the wedges as you go so that they cook evenly.

When the pork is ready, remove it from the barbecue and leave to rest, covered, for 10 minutes before carving. Cut the crackling with a sharp knife, arrange it on a platter with the pork and serve with the wedges.

SERVES 6–8

Asian pork ribs

1 kg (2 lb 4 oz) pork ribs, cut
    into sections of 4–5 ribs
3 tablespoons hoisin sauce
1 tablespoon Chinese rice wine
    or dry sherry
3 tablespoons soy sauce
2 garlic cloves, chopped
1 tablespoon oil

2 spring onions (scallions),
    finely chopped
2 teaspoons grated fresh ginger
600 g (1 lb 5 oz) baby bok choy
    (pak choy), leaves separated

boiled rice, to serve (optional)

Place the ribs in a non-metallic bowl. Combine the hoisin sauce, rice wine, soy sauce, garlic, 1 tablespoon oil, 2 tablespoons spring onion and the ginger. Pour over the ribs and marinate for at least 10 minutes, or overnight in the refrigerator.

Heat a barbecue grill plate and brush with oil. Remove the ribs from the marinade, reserving the marinade. Cook the ribs in batches, if necessary, 8–10 minutes on each side, or until cooked through, basting with the marinade during cooking.

Before the ribs are cooked, bring the reserved marinade to the boil in a pan (add 4 tablespoons of water if necessary). Boil for 2 minutes, then add the bok choy. Cover and cook for 1–2 minutes, or until just wilted. Serve the ribs with the bok choy, drizzle with the marinade and serve with rice, if desired.

SERVES 4

Ginger-orange pork

6 pork butterfly steaks
250 ml (9 oz/1 cup) ginger wine
150 g (5½ oz/½ cup) orange marmalade
2 tablespoons oil
1 tablespoon grated fresh ginger

Trim the pork steak of excess fat and sinew. Mix together the wine, marmalade, oil and ginger. Place the steaks in a shallow non-metallic dish and add the marinade. Store, covered with plastic wrap, in the fridge for at least 3 hours, turning occasionally. Drain, reserving the marinade.

Cook the pork on a hot, lightly oiled barbecue flat plate or grill for 5 minutes each side or until tender, turning once.

While the meat is cooking, place the reserved marinade in a small pan. Bring to the boil, reduce the heat and simmer for 5 minutes, or until the marinade has reduced and thickened slightly. Pour over the pork.

SERVES 6

NOTE: Steaks of uneven thickness may curl when cooked. Prevent this by leaving a layer of fat on the outside and making a few deep cuts in it prior to cooking. Remove before serving.

Roast rack of pork with chunky apple sauce

6 Granny Smith apples
90 g (3¼ oz/⅓ cup) sugar
3 tablespoons white vinegar
2 tablespoons finely shredded mint leaves
1 rack of pork with 6 ribs (about 1.6 kg/3 lb 8 oz)
1 tablespoon olive oil

Peel the apples, remove the seeds, and roughly dice the flesh. Simmer over low heat with the sugar, vinegar and 3 tablespoons of water in a small saucepan for 15 minutes, or until cooked through and just beginning to collapse. Remove the sauce from the heat and stir in the shredded mint.

Score the skin on the rack of pork in a large diamond pattern, rub the oil all over the pork, then rub 1 teaspoon salt into the skin.

Preheat a kettle or covered barbecue to medium indirect heat. Put the pork rack in the middle of the barbecue, cover it and roast for about 1 hour 20 minutes, or until the juices run clear when a skewer is inserted into the thickest part of the flesh.

When the pork is cooked, remove it from the barbecue, and leave it to rest, covered, for 10 minutes. Slice between the bones and serve with chunky apple sauce and roasted carrots, if desired.

SERVES 6

Pork with apple and onion wedges

2 pork fillets, about 400 g (14 oz) each
12 pitted prunes
2 green apples, cored, unpeeled, cut into wedges
2 red onions, cut into wedges
50 g (1¾ oz) butter, melted
2 teaspoons caster (superfine) sugar
125 ml (4 fl oz/½ cup) pouring (whipping) cream
2 tablespoons brandy
1 tablespoon chopped chives

Trim the pork of any excess fat and sinew and cut each fillet in half. Make a slit with a knife through the centre of each fillet and push 3 prunes into each one. Brush the pork, the apple and onion wedges with the melted butter and sprinkle the apple and onion with the caster sugar.

Brown the pork on a hot, lightly oiled barbecue flat plate. Add the apple and onion wedges. Cook, turning frequently, for 5–7 minutes, or until the pork is cooked through and the apple and onion pieces are softened. Remove the pork, apple and onion from the barbecue and keep warm.

Mix together the cream, brandy and chives in a saucepan. Transfer to the stovetop and simmer for 3 minutes, or until slightly thickened. Season.

Slice the meat and serve with the apple, onion wedges and brandy cream sauce.

SERVES 4

Honey-roasted pork fillet

1 tablespoon finely grated fresh ginger
6 garlic cloves
4 tablespoons soy sauce
2 tablespoons oil
2 kg (4 lb 8 oz) piece pork neck or blade roast
2 tablespoons honey

Mix the ginger, garlic, soy sauce and oil in a large non-metallic bowl. Put the pork in the marinade and turn to coat well, then cover and refrigerate overnight.

Remove the pork from the marinade, pour the marinade into a small saucepan and simmer it over low heat for 5 minutes or until it is slightly reduced. Stir the honey into the warm marinade and remove from the heat.

Preheat a kettle or covered barbecue to low–medium indirect heat, then put the pork in the middle of the barbecue and roast, covered, for 45 minutes or until cooked through. In the last 10 minutes of cooking, baste the roast all over with the reduced marinade. Remove the roast from the barbecue and put it on a tray, covered, to rest for 10 minutes. Carve the roast and serve it with any pan juices left in the tray.

SERVES 6–8

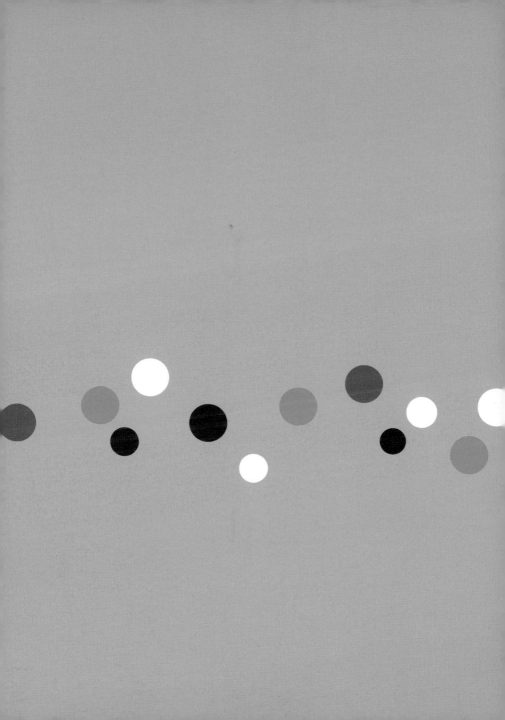

chicken

Mediterranean
chicken skewers

2 large chicken breast fillets, cut into 32 cubes
24 cherry tomatoes
6 cap mushrooms, cut into quarters
2 garlic cloves, crushed
zest of 1 lemon, grated
2 tablespoons lemon juice
2 tablespoons olive oil
1 tablespoon oregano leaves, chopped

Soak eight wooden skewers in water for 30 minutes. Thread a piece of chicken onto each skewer, followed by a tomato, then a piece of mushroom. Repeat twice for each skewer and finish with a piece of chicken. Put the skewers in a shallow, non-metallic dish.

Combine the garlic, lemon zest, lemon juice, olive oil and chopped oregano. Pour over the skewers and toss well. Marinate for at least 2 hours, or overnight.

Cook the skewers on a hot, lightly oiled barbecue grill or flat plate for 4 minutes on each side, basting occasionally, until the chicken is cooked and the tomatoes have shrivelled slightly. Serve immediately.

MAKES 8 SKEWERS

Spicy buffalo wings with ranch dressing

12 large chicken wings
2 teaspoons garlic salt
2 teaspoons onion powder
oil, for deep-frying
125 ml (4 fl oz/½ cup) tomato
   sauce (ketchup)
2 tablespoons worcestershire
   sauce
50 g (1¾ oz) butter, melted
Tabasco sauce, to taste

Ranch dressing
1 small garlic clove, crushed
185 g (6½ oz) mayonnaise
125 ml (4 fl oz/½ cup)
   buttermilk
2 tablespoons finely chopped
   flat-leaf (Italian) parsley
1 tablespoon chopped chives
1½ teaspoons lemon juice
1½ teaspoons dijon mustard
1 teaspoon onion powder

Remove and discard the tip of each chicken wing, then cut in half at the joint. Combine the garlic salt, onion powder and 2 teaspoons of ground black pepper, and rub the mixture into each chicken piece.

Deep-fry the chicken in batches over high heat for 2–3 minutes, then remove from the oil and drain on paper towels. Put the chicken in a non-metallic bowl with the combined tomato sauce, worcestershire sauce, butter and Tabasco and toss. Cover and refrigerate for at least 2 hours, or overnight.

To make the ranch dressing, mash the garlic and ¼ teaspoon salt. Add the mayonnaise, buttermilk, parsley, chives, lemon juice, mustard and onion powder and whisk together. Season, cover and refrigerate for at least 1 hour.

Preheat a barbecue flat plate to medium direct heat. Cook the chicken for 6–8 minutes on each side. Serve hot with the ranch dressing.

SERVES 4

Yakitori chicken burgers

4 chicken thigh fillets, trimmed
185 ml (6 fl oz/¾ cup) yakitori sauce
1 teaspoon cornflour (cornstarch)
oil, for brushing
4 soft hamburger buns, halved
80 g (2¾ oz/⅓ cup) Japanese mayonnaise (see Note)
80 g (2¾ oz) mizuna lettuce
1 Lebanese (short) cucumber, ends trimmed and shaved into ribbons
    with a vegetable peeler

Toss the chicken and yakitori sauce together in a bowl until the chicken fillets are well coated, then cover and refrigerate for 4 hours.

Drain the yakitori sauce from the chicken into a small saucepan and sprinkle it with the cornflour. Stir the cornflour into the marinade, bring the mixture to the boil and simmer, stirring frequently, for 5 minutes, or until it is thickened, then keep it warm.

Lightly brush the chargrill with oil, preheat it to low–medium direct heat and cook the chicken on the chargrill for 6–7 minutes on each side, or until it is cooked through. Toast the burger buns for about 1 minute on each side, or until they are marked and golden.

Spread some mayonnaise on the inside surface of each bun, cover the base with mizuna and cucumber ribbons, and top with the chicken. Spread some of the thickened marinade over the chicken and top with the other half of the bun.

SERVES 4

NOTE: Japanese mayonnaise will be available in larger supermarkets and Asian speciality stores. If you can't find it, use regular whole-egg mayonnaise instead.

Blackened Cajun spiced chicken

1½ tablespoons onion powder
1½ tablespoons garlic powder
2 teaspoons paprika
1 teaspoon white pepper
2 teaspoons dried thyme
½–1 teaspoon chilli powder
8 chicken drumsticks, scored

Combine the onion powder, garlic powder, paprika, white pepper, thyme, chilli powder and 1 teaspoon salt in a plastic bag. Place the drumsticks in the bag and shake until all the pieces are coated. Refrigerate the chicken for at least 30 minutes to allow the flavours to develop, or overnight if time permits.

Cook the chicken on a lightly oiled barbecue grill plate for 55–60 minutes, or until slightly blackened and cooked through. Brush lightly with some oil to prevent drying out during cooking.

SERVES 4

Honey chicken wings

12 chicken wings
4 tablespoons soy sauce
3 tablespoons sherry
3 tablespoons oil
1 garlic clove, crushed
3 tablespoons honey

Rinse the chicken wings, then give them a thorough pat with paper towels to dry them. Tuck the wing tips into the underside.

Put the chicken wings in a shallow non-metallic dish. Whisk together the soy sauce, sherry, oil and garlic, then pour all over the chicken wings. Cover with plastic wrap, then refrigerate for 2 hours.

Put the honey in a small saucepan over medium heat until it is heated enough for it to become brushing consistency.

Lightly grease a barbecue flat plate and heat it to high heat. Cook the chicken wings until tender and cooked through, turning occasionally—this should take about 12 minutes. Brush the wings with the warmed honey and cook for a further 2 minutes.

SERVES 4

Persian chicken skewers

2 teaspoons ground cardamom
1/2 teaspoon ground turmeric
1 teaspoon ground allspice
4 garlic cloves, crushed
3 tablespoons lemon juice
3 tablespoons olive oil
4 large chicken thigh fillets, excess fat removed
lemon wedges, to serve
plain yoghurt, to serve

To make the marinade, whisk together the cardamom, turmeric, allspice, garlic, lemon juice and oil. Season.

Cut each chicken thigh fillet into 3–4 cm (1¼–1½ inch) cubes. Toss the cubes in the spice marinade. Cover and refrigerate overnight.

Thread the chicken onto metal skewers and cook on a hot, lightly oiled barbecue grill or flat plate for 4 minutes on each side, or until the chicken is cooked through. Serve with lemon wedges and plain yoghurt.

SERVES 4

Drumsticks in tomato and mango chutney

8 chicken drumsticks, scored
1 tablespoon mustard powder
2 tablespoons tomato sauce (ketchup)
1 tablespoon sweet mango chutney
1 teaspoon worcestershire sauce
1 tablespoon dijon mustard
30 g (1 oz/¼ cup) raisins
1 tablespoon oil

Toss the chicken in the mustard powder and season. Combine the tomato sauce, mango chutney, worcestershire sauce, mustard, raisins and oil. Spoon over the chicken and toss well. Marinate for at least 2 hours, turning once.

Cook the chicken on a hot lightly oiled barbecue flat plate for about 20 minutes, or until cooked through.

SERVES 4

Chicken tikka with garlic naan and apple raita

100 g (3½ oz/⅓ cup) tikka paste
60 g (2¼ oz/¼ cup) Greek-style
    yoghurt
600 g (1 lb 5 oz) chicken breast
    fillet, cut into 3 cm (1¼ inch)
    cubes
2 small red onions, quartered
oil, for brushing
2 tablespoons chopped
    coriander (cilantro) leaves

Apple raita
1 green apple, grated
2 teaspoons lemon juice
60 g (2¼ oz/¼ cup) sour cream
3 tablespoons chopped mint
    leaves

Garlic naan
1 garlic clove, crushed
2 tablespoons butter, softened
4 plain naan

Combine the tikka paste and yoghurt in a bowl. Add the chicken and turn until it evenly coated. Cover with plastic wrap and refrigerate for 4 hours, or overnight.

To make the raita, put the grated apple, lemon juice, sour cream and mint in a small bowl and stir to combine. Cover the bowl and refrigerate until required. Soak four wooden skewers in cold water for 1 hour.

Mash the crushed garlic and butter together and brush one side of each piece of naan with about 2 teaspoons of garlic butter.

Preheat the barbecue grill plate to low–medium direct heat. Thread the chicken and onion pieces onto the skewers and cook on the flat plate for 5–6 minutes on each side. Grill the naan, buttered-side down, for 1–2 minutes, or until golden and marked. Turn and grill for a further 1 minute on the other side.

Sprinkle the skewers with the coriander. Serve with the garlic naan and apple raita.

SERVES 4

Crispy chicken wings

12 chicken wings
3 tablespoons soy sauce
3 tablespoons hoisin sauce
125 g (4½ oz/½ cup) tomato sauce (ketchup)
2 tablespoons honey
1 tablespoon soft brown sugar
1 tablespoon cider vinegar
2 garlic cloves, crushed
¼ teaspoon Chinese five-spice
2 teaspoons sesame oil

Tuck the chicken wing tips to the underside and place in a non-metallic bowl.

Mix together all the remaining ingredients and pour over the wings, tossing to coat. Cover and leave in the fridge for at least 2 hours, turning occasionally. Drain, reserving the marinade.

Cook the wings on a hot, lightly oiled barbecue grill or flat plate for 5 minutes, or until cooked through, brushing with the reserved marinade several times.

SERVES 6

Thai spiced chicken with potato rosti

600 g (1 lb 5 oz) chicken breast
   fillet, cut into strips
1 tablespoon chopped lemon
   grass
2 tablespoons lime juice
1½ tablespoons oil
2 garlic cloves, crushed
1 tablespoon grated fresh
   ginger

2 teaspoons sweet chilli sauce
2 spring onions (scallions),
   chopped
1 lime, cut into 6 wedges

Potato rosti
600 g (1 lb 5 oz) potatoes
3 tablespoons plain (all-
   purpose) flour
1 egg, lightly beaten

Put the chicken in a shallow, non-metallic dish. Mix together the lemon grass, lime juice, oil, garlic, ginger, sweet chilli sauce and spring onion. Pour over the chicken pieces, cover and refrigerate for at least 2 hours.

To make the potato rosti, peel and grate the potatoes. Squeeze the excess moisture from the potato with your hands until it feels quite dry. Mix the potato with the flour and egg and season well. Divide into six equal portions. Cook on a hot, lightly oiled barbecue flat plate for 10 minutes, or until golden brown on both sides, flattening them down with the back of a spatula during cooking.

Drain the chicken and reserve the marinade. Cook on a barbecue grill or flat plate for 3 minutes each side, or until tender and golden brown. Brush with the reserved marinade while cooking. Serve with the rosti and a squeeze of lime juice.

SERVES 6

Honey mustard chicken

175 g (6 oz/½ cup) honey
60 g (2¼ oz/¼ cup) dijon mustard
2 tablespoons oil
2 tablespoons white wine vinegar
3 garlic cloves, crushed
2 tablespoons chopped flat-leaf (Italian) parsley leaves
1.8 kg (4 lb) chicken, cut into 10 serving pieces

Put the honey, mustard, oil, vinegar, garlic, parsley and ¼ teaspoon freshly ground black pepper in a large non-metallic bowl. Mix together well. Set aside 3 tablespoons of the marinade to baste the chicken during cooking. Add the chicken pieces to the rest of the marinade and turn to coat. Cover and refrigerate for at least 4 hours, or overnight.

Preheat a covered or kettle barbecue to medium indirect heat and cook the chicken pieces for 20–30 minutes, or until they are cooked through. The breast pieces may take as little as 15 minutes, while dark meat will take longer. Baste the chicken with the reserved marinade during the last 5–8 minutes of cooking, but no earlier or it is likely to burn.

SERVES 4–6

Lebanese chicken

250 g (9 oz/1 cup) plain yoghurt
2 teaspoons soft brown sugar
4 garlic cloves, crushed
3 teaspoons ground cumin
1½ teaspoons ground coriander
1 small handful flat-leaf (Italian) parsley, chopped
3 tablespoons lemon juice
1 x 1.8 kg (4 lb) chicken, cut into 10 serving pieces
cooking oil spray

Put the yoghurt, brown sugar, garlic, cumin, coriander, chopped parsley and lemon juice in a large non-metallic bowl and mix together. Add the chicken pieces to the marinade and turn to coat. Cover and refrigerate for at least 2 hours, or overnight.

Lightly spray the barbecue flat plate with oil, then preheat the barbecue to medium direct heat. Remove the chicken pieces from the marinade and season. Cook the chicken pieces on the flat plate, turning frequently, for 20–30 minutes, or until cooked through.

SERVES 4–6

Five-spice roast chicken

1.8 kg (4 lb) chicken
1 tablespoon soy sauce
2 garlic cloves, crushed
1 teaspoon finely grated fresh ginger
1 tablespoon honey
1 tablespoon rice wine
1 teaspoon Chinese five-spice
1 tablespoon peanut oil

Wash the chicken and pat it thoroughly dry inside and out with paper towels. Whisk the soy sauce, garlic, ginger, honey, rice wine and five-spice together in a small bowl and brush all over the chicken. Put the chicken on a wire rack over a baking tray and refrigerate, uncovered, for at least 8 hours, or overnight.

Preheat a kettle or covered barbecue to medium indirect heat and put a drip tray under the rack. Brush the chicken liberally with the peanut oil and put it breast-side up in the middle of the barbecue over the drip tray. Cover the barbecue and roast the chicken for 1 hour 10 minutes, or until the juices run clear when you pierce it with a skewer between the thigh and body. Check the chicken every so often, and if it appears to be over-browning, cover it loosely with foil. Leave it to rest, covered, for 10 minutes before carving and serving.

SERVES 4

Lime and coriander chargrilled chicken

3 teaspoons finely grated fresh ginger
25 g (1 oz) chopped coriander (cilantro) leaves
1½ teaspoons grated lime zest
4 tablespoons lime juice
4 skinless chicken breast fillets (about 750 g/1lb 10 oz), trimmed
2 tablespoons oil
3 zucchini (courgettes), cut into wedges
4 large flat mushrooms, stalks trimmed

Combine the ginger, coriander, lime zest and 2 tablespoons of the lime juice. Spread 2 teaspoons of the herb mixture over each fillet and season well. Marinate for 1 hour. Combine the remaining herb mixture with the remaining lime juice in a screwtop jar. Set aside until needed.

Heat a barbecue grill plate to medium and lightly brush with oil. Brush the zucchini and mushrooms with the remaining oil. Place the chicken on the grill plate and cook on each side for 4–5 minutes, or until cooked through. Add the vegetables during the last 5 minutes of cooking, and turn frequently until browned on the outside and just softened. Cover with foil until ready to serve.

Cut the chicken fillets into long thick strips. Drizzle the dressing over the chicken and serve with the chargrilled vegetables.

SERVES 4

seafood

Swordfish shish kebabs with herb yoghurt

800 g (1 lb 12 oz) skinless
    swordfish fillet, cut into 3 cm
    (1¼ inch) chunks
4 tablespoons lemon juice
4 tablespoons olive oil
3 bay leaves
16 cherry tomatoes
2 small red onions, each cut into
    8 wedges
2 small red or orange capsicums
    (peppers), deseeded and cut
    into 8 chunks

Lemon and herb yoghurt
200 g (7 oz) Greek-style yoghurt
3 teaspoons lemon juice
pinch of paprika
1 tablespoon finely chopped
    mint
1 tablespoon finely chopped
    flat-leaf (Italian) parsley

Put the chunks of swordfish in a non-metallic bowl with the lemon juice, olive oil and bay leaves. Toss to mix, cover and refrigerate for at least 2 hours.

To make the lemon and herb yoghurt, whisk together all the ingredients in a small bowl. Refrigerate until needed.

Thread five chunks of fish, two cherry tomatoes, two pieces of onion and two pieces of capsicum onto each of the eight metal skewers, alternating between the fish and the vegetables.

Cook the kebabs on a barbecue flat plate for 8–10 minutes. Baste with the remaining marinade as they cook. The fish should be firm and opaque.

Serve the kebabs drizzled with the yoghurt dressing and couscous, if desired.

SERVES 4

Coriander prawns

8 large raw prawns (shrimp)
1 tablespoon sweet chilli sauce
1 teaspoon ground coriander
125 ml (4 fl oz/½ cup) olive oil
4 tablespoons lime juice
3 garlic cloves, crushed
1 tomato, peeled, seeded and chopped
2 tablespoons chopped coriander (cilantro)

Remove the heads from the prawns and, with a sharp knife, cut the prawns in half lengthways, leaving the tails attached. Pull out each dark vein.

Mix together the sweet chilli sauce and ground coriander with half the olive oil, half the lime juice and half the garlic. Add the prawns, toss to coat, then cover and refrigerate for 30 minutes.

Meanwhile, to make the dressing, mix the remaining olive oil, lime juice and garlic in a bowl with the chopped tomato and coriander.

Drain the prawns, reserving the marinade. Cook, cut side down, on a hot, lightly oiled barbecue grill or flat plate for 1–2 minutes each side, or until cooked through, brushing occasionally with the marinade. Spoon a little of the dressing over the prawns and season well before serving.

SERVES 4

Tuna burgers with herbed mayonnaise

4 garlic cloves, crushed
2 egg yolks
250 ml (9 fl oz/1 cup) light olive
  oil
3 tablespoons chopped flat-leaf
  (Italian) parsley
1 tablespoon chopped dill
2 teaspoons dijon mustard
1 tablespoon lemon juice
1 tablespoon red wine vinegar

1 tablespoon baby capers in
  brine, drained
4 anchovy fillets in oil, drained
4 x 150 g (5½ oz) tuna steaks
2 tablespoons olive oil
2 red onions, thinly sliced
4 large round bread rolls,
  halved and buttered
100 g (3½ oz) mixed lettuce
  leaves

Put the garlic and egg yolks in a food processor and process for 10 seconds. With the motor running, add the oil in a very thin, slow stream. When the mixture starts to thicken, pour the oil a little faster until it has all been added and the mixture is thick and creamy. Add the parsley, dill, mustard, lemon juice, vinegar, capers and anchovies, and process until the mixture is smooth. Refrigerate until you need.

Preheat the barbecue grill plate to high direct heat. Brush the tuna steaks with 1 tablespoon of olive oil and cook for 2 minutes on each side, or until almost cooked through. Add the remaining olive oil to the onion, toss to separate and coat the rings, and cook on the flat plate for 2 minutes, or until the onion is soft and caramelized. Toast the rolls, buttered-side down, on the grill plate for 1 minute, or until marked and golden.

Put some lettuce, a tuna steak, some of the onion and a dollop of herbed mayonnaise on one half of each roll. Season and top with the other half of the roll.

SERVES 4

Tuna skewers with Moroccan spices

800 g (1 lb 12 oz) tuna steaks,
  cut into cubes
2 tablespoons olive oil
½ teaspoon ground cumin
2 teaspoons grated lemon zest
couscous, to serve (optional)

Chermoula
3 teaspoons ground cumin
½ teaspoon ground coriander

2 teaspoons paprika
pinch of cayenne pepper
4 garlic cloves, crushed
15 g (½ oz) chopped flat-leaf
  (Italian) parsley
30 g (1 oz) chopped coriander
  (cilantro) leaves
4 tablespoons lemon juice
125 ml (4 fl oz/½ cup) olive oil

Put the tuna in a shallow non-metallic dish. Combine the olive oil, ground cumin and lemon zest and pour over the tuna. Toss to coat and leave to marinate for 10 minutes.

To make the chermoula, place the cumin, coriander, paprika and cayenne in a frying pan and cook over medium heat for 30 seconds, or until fragrant. Combine with the remaining ingredients and leave for the flavours to develop.

Thread the tuna onto metal skewers. Cook on a hot, lightly oiled barbecue grill or flat plate until cooked to your taste (about 1 minute on each side for rare and 2 minutes for medium). Serve the skewers with the chermoula drizzled over and some couscous, if desired.

SERVES 4

Honey and lime prawn kebabs with salsa

32 prawns (shrimp), peeled and
  deveined, tails intact
3 tablespoons clear runny honey
1 small red chilli, deseeded and
  finely chopped
2 tablespoons olive oil
zest and juice of 2 limes
1 large garlic clove, crushed
2 cm (¾ inch) piece of fresh
  ginger, finely grated
1 tablespoon chopped
  coriander (cilantro) leaves

Salsa
2 tomatoes
1 small just-ripe mango, diced
½ small red onion, diced
1 small red chilli, deseeded and
  finely chopped
zest and juice of 1 lime
2 tablespoons chopped
  coriander (cilantro) leaves

Put the prawns in a non-metallic dish. Whisk the honey, chilli, olive oil, lime zest and juice, garlic, ginger and coriander together, then pour over the prawns. Toss well. Cover and refrigerate for at least 3 hours. Meanwhile, soak eight bamboo skewers in water for 30 minutes.

To make the salsa, score a cross in the base of each tomato. Cover with boiling water for 30 seconds, then plunge into cold water. Peel the skin away from the cross. Dice the tomatoes, discarding the cores and saving any juice.

In a bowl, mix the tomatoes and juice with the mango, red onion, chilli, lime zest and juice and coriander.

Preheat a barbecue flat plate to high. Thread four prawns onto each skewer. Cook for 4 minutes, turning halfway through cooking. Baste with the leftover marinade as they cook. Serve the kebabs with the salsa and some rice.

SERVES 4

Sweet chilli octopus

1.5 kg (3 lb 5 oz) baby octopus
250 ml (9 fl oz/1 cup) sweet chilli sauce
4 tablespoons lime juice
4 tablespoons fish sauce
60 g (2¼ oz/⅓ cup) soft brown sugar
lime wedges, to serve

Cut off the octopus heads, below the eyes, with a sharp knife. Discard the heads and guts. Push the beaks out with your index finger, remove and discard. Wash the octopus thoroughly under running water and drain on crumpled paper towels. If the octopus tentacles are large, cut into quarters.

Mix together the sweet chilli sauce, lime juice, fish sauce and sugar.

Cook the octopus on a very hot, lightly oiled barbecue grill or flat plate, turning often, for 3–4 minutes, or until it just changes colour. Brush with a quarter of the sauce during cooking. Take care not to overcook the octopus or it will toughen. Serve immediately with the remaining sauce and lime wedges.

SERVES 4

Scallop and fish rosemary skewers

2 tablespoons marjoram leaves
1 tablespoon lemon juice
4 tablespoons olive oil, plus
    extra, for brushing
1 small handful flat-leaf
    (Italian) parsley, chopped
8 long firm rosemary branches

600 g (1 lb 5 oz) firm white fish
    fillets, cut into 3 cm (1¼ inch)
    cubes
16 scallops with roe attached
lemon wedges, to serve

Pound the marjoram leaves in a mortar and pestle with a little salt until the mixture forms a paste. Add the lemon juice, then stir in the olive oil and parsley, and season to taste.

Pull the leaves off the rosemary branches, leaving just a tuft at the end of each stem. Thread three pieces of fish and two scallops alternately onto each rosemary skewer, brush with a little olive oil and season well.

Preheat the barbecue flat plate to medium direct heat. Cook the skewers for 3–4 minutes on each side, or until the fish is cooked through.

Serve the skewers with lemon wedges and the dressing.

SERVES 4

Piri piri prawns

1 kg (2 lb 4 oz) large raw
    prawns (shrimp)
4 long red chillies, seeded
185 ml (6 fl oz/¾ cup) white
    wine vinegar

2 large garlic cloves, chopped
6–8 small red chillies, chopped
125 ml (4 fl oz/½ cup) olive oil
150 g (5½ oz) mixed lettuce
    leaves

Remove the heads from the prawns and slice them down the back without cutting right through, leaving the tail intact. Open out each prawn and remove the dark vein, then refrigerate the prepared prawns until required.

To make the sauce, put the long chillies in a saucepan with the vinegar and simmer over medium–high heat for 5 minutes, or until the chillies are soft. Let the mixture cool slightly, then put the chillies and 3 tablespoons of the vinegar in a food processor. Add the garlic and chopped small chillies, and blend until the mixture is smooth. While the motor is running, gradually add the oil and remaining vinegar to the food processor.

Put the prawns in the marinade, making sure they are well coated, then cover and refrigerate for 30 minutes.

Remove the prawns from the marinade. Bring the marinade to the boil and simmer for 5 minutes, or until it is slightly thickened and reduced.

Lightly oil the barbecue grill plate and heat it to high direct heat. Cook the prawns, basting with the marinade, for 2–3 minutes on each side, or until cooked through. Arrange the lettuce on four plates, top with the prawns and serve immediately with the chilli sauce.

SERVES 4

Fish tikka

Marinade
500 g (9 oz/2 cups) Greek-style
   yoghurt
2 red Asian shallots, finely
   chopped
1 tablespoon grated fresh ginger
2 garlic cloves, crushed
2 tablespoons lemon juice
1 teaspoon ground coriander
1 tablespoon garam masala
1 teaspoon paprika
1 teaspoon chilli powder
2 tablespoons tomato paste
   (concentrated purée)

500 g (1 lb 2 oz) skinless flake
2 onions, each cut into 8 chunks
2 small red capsicums (peppers),
   each deseeded and cut into
   8 chunks
1 Lebanese (short) cucumber,
   peeled and diced
2 tablespoons chopped
   coriander (cilantro) leaves
lemon wedges, for serving

Fish substitution
sea bream, snapper, grouper,
orange roughy, sea bass

To make the marinade, mix half of the yoghurt, all of the remaining marinade ingredients and 1 teaspoon salt together in a shallow non-metallic dish.

Cut the fish into 24 bite-sized pieces. On each metal skewer, thread three pieces of fish and two chunks each of onion and capsicum, alternating as you go. Turn the skewers in the dish containing the marinade so that all the fish and vegetables are well coated. Cover and refrigerate for at least 1 hour.

Preheat the barbecue flat plate. Cook the skewers for about 5 minutes, or until the fish is firm and opaque.

Meanwhile, stir the cucumber and coriander into the remaining yoghurt. Serve the fish with the yoghurt and lemon wedges.

SERVES 4

Chargrilled
baby octopus

2 kg (4 lb 8 oz) baby octopus
375 ml (13 fl oz/1½ cups) red wine
3 tablespoons balsamic vinegar
2 tablespoons soy sauce
125 ml (4 fl oz/½ cup) sweet chilli sauce
50 g (1¾ oz) Thai basil leaves, to serve

Clean the octopus, taking care not to break the ink sacs. Place the octopus, red wine and balsamic vinegar in a large, non-aluminium saucepan and bring to the boil. Reduce the heat and simmer for 15 minutes, or until just tender. Drain and transfer to a bowl. Add the soy sauce and sweet chilli sauce.

Heat a barbecue grill plate to high and cook the octopus until it is sticky and slightly charred. Serve on a bed of Thai basil leaves.

SERVES 4

Asian-style seafood

500 g (1 lb 2 oz) prawns (shrimp), peeled and
  deveined, tails intact
300 g (10½ oz) scallop meat
500 g (1 lb 2 oz) baby squid, cleaned, cut into quarters
500 g (1 lb 2 oz) baby octopus, cleaned
250 ml (9 oz/1 cup) sweet chilli sauce
1 tablespoon fish sauce
2 tablespoons lime juice
3 tablespoons peanut oil
lime wedges, to serve

Put the prawns, scallops, squid and octopus in a shallow non-metallic bowl. In a separate bowl, combine the sweet chilli sauce, fish sauce, lime juice and 1 tablespoon of the peanut oil. Pour the mixture over the seafood and mix gently to coat. Allow to marinate for 1 hour. Drain the seafood well and reserve the marinade.

Heat the remaining oil on a barbecue flat plate. Cook the seafood, in batches if necessary, over high heat for 3–5 minutes, or until tender. Drizzle each batch with a little of the leftover marinade during cooking. Serve with wedges of lime and rice, if desired.

SERVES 6

Chermoula prawns

1 kg (2 lb 4 oz) raw medium
    prawns (shrimp)
3 teaspoons hot paprika
2 teaspoons ground cumin
30 g (1 oz) flat-leaf (Italian)
    parsley

15 g (½ oz) coriander (cilantro)
    leaves
100 ml (3½ fl oz) lemon juice
145 ml (5 fl oz) olive oil
lemon wedges, to serve
couscous, to serve (optional)

Peel the prawns, leaving the tails intact, and discard the heads. Gently pull out the dark vein from the backs, starting at the head end. Put the prawns in a bowl.

Dry-fry the paprika and cumin in a frying pan for about 1 minute, or until fragrant. Remove from the heat.

Blend or process the spices, parsley, coriander, lemon juice and 125 ml (4 fl oz/ ½ cup) of the oil until finely chopped. Season. Pour over the prawns and mix well, then cover with plastic wrap and refrigerate for 10 minutes. Heat a barbecue grill plate to hot.

Cook the prawns on the grill plate for about 3–4 minutes, or until cooked through, turning and brushing with extra marinade while cooking (take care not to overcook). Serve the prawns with a wedge of lemon and couscous, if desired.

SERVES 4

Squid with picada dressing

500 g (1 lb 2 oz) small squid

Picada dressing
2 tablespoons extra virgin olive oil
2 tablespoons finely chopped flat-leaf (Italian) parsley
1 garlic clove, crushed
¼ teaspoon cracked black pepper

To clean the squid, gently pull the tentacles away from the hood (the intestines should come away at the same time). Remove the intestines from the tentacles by cutting under the eyes, then remove the beak, if it remains in the centre of the tentacles, by pushing up with your index finger. Pull away the soft bone.

Rub the hoods under cold running water and the skin should come away easily. Wash the hoods and tentacles and drain well. Place in a bowl, add ¼ teaspoon salt and mix well. Cover and refrigerate for about 30 minutes.

To make the picada dressing, whisk together the olive oil, parsley, garlic, pepper and some salt.

Cook the squid hoods in small batches on a very hot, lightly oiled barbecue flat plate for 2–3 minutes, or until white and tender. Cook the squid tentacles, turning to brown all over, for 1 minute, or until they curl up. Serve hot, drizzled with the picada dressing.

SERVES 6

Swordfish with tomato butter

100 g (3½ oz) butter, softened
50 g (1¾ oz/⅓ cup) semi-dried (sun-blushed) tomatoes, finely chopped
2 tablespoons baby capers in brine, drained and crushed

1½ tablespoons shredded basil leaves
2 garlic cloves, crushed
1 tablespoon extra virgin olive oil
4 swordfish steaks

Put the butter in a bowl with the tomato, capers, basil and two cloves of crushed garlic, and mash it all together. Shape the flavoured butter into a log, then wrap in baking paper and twist the ends to close them off. Refrigerate until the butter is firm, then cut into 1 cm (½ inch) slices and leave, covered, at room temperature until needed.

Preheat a barbecue grill plate to high direct heat. Brush the swordfish steaks with the remaining oil and cook for 2–3 minutes on each side, or until just cooked through. Put a piece of the tomato butter on top of each steak as soon as it comes off the barbecue and season to taste. Serve the fish with asparagus, if desired.

SERVES 4

King prawns with dill mayonnaise

Marinade
125 ml (4 fl oz/½ cup) olive oil
4 tablespoons lemon juice
2 tablespoons wholegrain
   mustard
2 tablespoons honey
2 tablespoons chopped dill

16–20 raw king prawns (shrimp)

Dill mayonnaise
185 g (6½ oz/¾ cup)
   mayonnaise
2 tablespoons chopped dill
1½ tablespoons lemon juice
1 gherkin, finely chopped
1 teaspoon chopped capers
1 garlic clove, crushed

To make the marinade, combine the olive oil, lemon juice, mustard, honey and dill, pour over the unpeeled prawns and coat well. Cover and refrigerate for at least 2 hours, turning occasionally.

To make the dill mayonnaise, whisk together the mayonnaise, dill, lemon juice, gherkin, capers and garlic. Cover and refrigerate.

Cook the drained prawns on a hot, lightly oiled barbecue grill or flat plate in batches for 4 minutes, turning frequently until pink and cooked through. Serve with the mayonnaise.

SERVES 4

Malaysian
barbecued seafood

1 onion, grated
4 garlic cloves, chopped
5 cm (2 inch) piece of fresh
  ginger, grated
3 stems lemon grass (white part
  only), chopped
2 teaspoons ground or grated
  fresh turmeric
1 teaspoon shrimp paste

4 tablespoons vegetable oil
¼ teaspoon salt
4 calamari tubes
2 thick white boneless fish fillets
8 raw king prawns (shrimp)
banana leaves, to serve
2 limes, cut into wedges
strips of lime zest, to garnish
mint leaves, to garnish

Combine the onion, garlic, ginger, lemon grass, turmeric, shrimp paste, oil and salt in a small food processor. Process in short bursts until the mixture forms a paste.

Cut the calamari in half lengthways and lay it on the bench with the soft inside facing up. Score a very fine honeycomb pattern into the soft side, taking care not to cut all the way through, and then cut into large pieces. Wash all the seafood under cold running water and pat dry with paper towels. Brush lightly with the spice paste, then place on a tray, cover and refrigerate for 15 minutes.

Lightly oil a barbecue grill plate to high heat. When the plate is hot, arrange the fish fillets and prawns on the plate. Cook, turning once only, for about 3 minutes each side or until the fish flesh is just firm and the prawns turn bright pink to orange. Add the calamari pieces and cook for 2 minutes or until the flesh turns white and rolls up. Take care not to overcook the seafood.

Arrange the seafood on a platter lined with the banana leaves, add the lime wedges and serve immediately, garnished with strips of lime zest and some fresh mint.

SERVES 4

Lobster with burnt butter sauce and grilled lemon

150 g (5½ oz) butter
3 tablespoons lemon juice
2 tablespoons chopped flat-leaf (Italian) parsley
1 small garlic clove, crushed
8 lobster tails in the shell
2 lemons, cut into wedges

Melt the butter in a small saucepan over medium heat and cook for 3 minutes, or until it begins to brown. Lower the heat, and cook the butter for a further 2 minutes, or until it is a dark, golden brown. Remove the pan from the heat, add the lemon juice, parsley and garlic, and season.

Cut the lobster tails lengthways and remove any digestive tract, but leave the meat in the shell.

Preheat a barbecue grill plate to medium direct heat and brush the exposed lobster meat with lots of the butter mixture. Cook the lobster tails, cut-side down, on the grill plate for 6 minutes, then turn and cook for a further 3–5 minutes, or until the shells turn bright red.

Meanwhile, put the lemon wedges on the hottest part of the chargrill and cook for 1 minute on each side, or until marked and heated through. Arrange the lobster on a serving plate and serve with the grilled lemon wedges and the rest of the warm brown butter as a dipping sauce.

SERVES 8

Crab with Singapore-style pepper sauce

2 kg (4 lb 8 oz) blue crabs
150 g (5½ oz) butter
2 tablespoons finely chopped garlic
1 tablespoon finely chopped fresh ginger
1 small red chilli, seeded and finely chopped
3 tablespoons ground black pepper
2 tablespoons dark soy sauce
2 tablespoons oyster sauce
1 tablespoon palm sugar or soft brown sugar
1 spring onion (scallion), green part only, sliced thinly on the diagonal

Pull back the apron and remove the top shell from each crab. Remove the intestine and the grey feathery gills, then use a sharp knife to cut the crab in half lengthways, leaving the legs attached. Crack the thick part of the legs with the back of a heavy knife or crab crackers to make it easier to extract the meat.

Heat a barbecue flat plate or grill plate to medium–high direct heat. Cook the crabs for 5–8 minutes on each side, or until orange and cooked through.

Heat a wok over medium heat (you'll need to do this on the stovetop if you don't have a wok burner on your barbecue), and stir-fry the butter, garlic, ginger, chilli and pepper for 30 seconds or until fragrant. Add the combined soy and oyster sauces and sugar and simmer for 1 minute or until glossy.

Toss the cooked crab in the sauce until completely coated, then arrange on a serving dish and sprinkle with the spring onion.

SERVES 4–6

Salmon cutlets with sweet cucumber dressing

2 small Lebanese (short) cucumbers, peeled,
  deseeded and finely diced
1 red onion, finely chopped
1 red chilli, finely chopped
2 tablespoons pickled ginger, shredded
2 tablespoons rice vinegar
1/2 teaspoon sesame oil
4 salmon cutlets
1 sheet toasted nori (dried seaweed),
  cut into thin strips

Fish substitution
ocean trout cutlets

Combine the cucumber, onion, chilli, ginger, rice vinegar and sesame oil in a bowl.
Cover and stand at room temperature.

Preheat a barbecue flat plate and lightly brush it with oil. Cook the salmon on the
barbecue for about 2 minutes on each side, or until cooked—it should be still just
pink in the centre.

Serve the salmon topped with the cucumber dressing, then sprinkle with strips of
toasted nori.

SERVES 4

Swordfish with anchovy and caper sauce

Sauce
1 large garlic clove
1 tablespoon capers, rinsed and finely chopped
50 g (1¾ oz) anchovy fillets, finely chopped
1 tablespoon finely chopped rosemary or dried oregano
finely grated zest and juice of ½ lemon

4 tablespoons extra virgin olive oil
1 large tomato, finely chopped

4 swordfish steaks
1 tablespoon extra virgin olive oil
crusty Italian bread, to serve

Put the garlic in a mortar and pestle with a little salt and crush it. To make the sauce, mix together the garlic, capers, anchovies, rosemary or oregano, lemon zest and juice, oil and tomato. Leave for 10 minutes.

Preheat a barbecue grill plate to very hot. Using paper towels, pat the swordfish dry and lightly brush with the olive oil. Season.

Cook the swordfish over high heat for about 2 minutes on each side, or until just cooked—the flesh should be opaque.

If the cooked swordfish is a little oily, drain on paper towels, then place on serving plates and drizzle with the sauce. Serve with Italian bread.

SERVES 4

Red mullet with herb sauce

4 x 200 g (7 oz) red mullet
3 tablespoons lemon juice
3 tablespoons olive oil
flat-leaf (Italian) parsley, to
    garnish
lemon wedges, to serve

Herb sauce
100 g (3½ oz) English spinach
3 tablespoons olive oil
1 tablespoon white wine
    vinegar

1 tablespoon chopped flat-leaf
    (Italian) parsley
1 tablespoon chopped chives
1 tablespoon chopped chervil
1 tablespoon finely chopped
    capers
2 anchovy fillets, finely chopped
1 hard-boiled egg, finely
    chopped

Preheat the barbecue flat plate. Make a few deep slashes in the thickest part of each fish. Pat the fish dry and season inside and out. Drizzle with a little lemon juice and olive oil. Cook for 4–5 minutes each side, or until the fish flakes. Baste with the lemon juice and oil during cooking.

To make the sauce, put the spinach in a large saucepan with just the water clinging to the leaves. Cover the pan and steam the spinach for 2 minutes, or until just wilted. Drain, cool and squeeze with your hands to get rid of the excess liquid. Finely chop. Mix with the oil, vinegar, herbs, capers, anchovy and egg in a food processor. Spoon the sauce onto a plate and place the fish on top. Sprinkle with parsley to garnish and serve with lemon wedges.

SERVES 4

vegetarian

Baby potatoes

750 g (1 lb 10 oz) baby potatoes, unpeeled
2 tablespoons olive oil
2 tablespoons thyme leaves
2 teaspoons crushed sea salt

Cut any large potatoes in half so that they are all the same size for even cooking. Boil the potatoes until just tender. Drain and lightly dry with paper towels.

Put the potatoes in a large bowl and add the oil and thyme. Toss gently and leave for 1 hour.

Lightly oil a barbecue flat plate and preheat to high direct heat. Cook the potatoes for 15 minutes, turning frequently and brushing with the remaining oil and thyme mixture, until golden brown. Sprinkle with salt to serve.

SERVES 6

NOTE: The potatoes can be left in the marinade for up to 2 hours before barbecuing, but should be served as soon as they are cooked.

Corn in the husk

8 fresh young corn cobs
125 ml (4 fl oz/½ cup) olive oil
6 garlic cloves, chopped
4 tablespoons chopped flat-leaf (Italian) parsley
butter, to serve

Peel back the corn husks, leaving them intact. Pull off the white silks, then wash the corn and pat dry with paper towels.

Combine the olive oil, garlic, parsley and some salt and black pepper and brush over each cob. Pull up the husks and tie together at the top with string. Steam over boiling water for 5 minutes, then pat dry.

Cook on a hot, lightly oiled barbecue grill or flat plate for 20 minutes, turning regularly. Spray with water during the cooking to keep the corn moist. Serve hot with knobs of butter.

SERVES 8

Asparagus with salsa

3 eggs
2 tablespoons milk
1 tablespoon olive oil
2 corn cobs
1 small red onion, diced
1 red capsicum (pepper), finely chopped
2 tablespoons chopped thyme
2 tablespoons olive oil, extra
2 tablespoons balsamic vinegar
24 asparagus spears
1 tablespoon macadamia oil
toasted bread, to serve

Beat the eggs and milk to combine. Heat the oil in a non-stick frying pan, add the egg and cook over a medium heat until just set. Flip and cook the other side. Remove and allow to cool, then roll up and cut into thick slices.

Cook the corn on a barbecue grill plate until tender. Set aside to cool slightly, then slice off the corn kernels. Combine the corn, onion, capsicum, thyme, olive oil and balsamic vinegar.

Trim off any woody ends from the asparagus, lightly brush with macadamia oil and cook on the grill until tender. Serve the asparagus topped with a little salsa and the finely shredded egg, accompanied by toasted bread.

SERVES 4–6

Eggplant with lemon pesto

2 large eggplants (aubergines), cut into 1.5 cm (⅝ inch) slices
  or 8 small eggplants (aubergines), halved lengthways
160 ml (5¼ fl oz/⅔ cup) extra virgin olive oil
60 g (2¼ oz) basil leaves
20 g (¾ oz) flat-leaf (Italian) parsley
50 g (1¾ oz/⅓ cup) pine nuts, toasted
1½ garlic cloves
60 g (2¼ oz) grated parmesan cheese
grated zest of 1 lemon
3 tablespoons lemon juice

Brush both sides of the eggplant slices with 2 tablespoons of extra virgin olive oil.

Heat a barbecue grill plate until hot. Cook the eggplant slices for 3 minutes, or until golden and cooked through on both sides. Cover the eggplant to keep warm.

Place the basil, parsley, pine nuts, garlic, parmesan, lemon zest and lemon juice in a food processor, and blend together. Slowly add the remaining olive oil and process until the mixture forms a smooth paste. Season.

Stack the eggplant on a platter, drizzling some pesto between each layer. Serve immediately.

SERVES 4–6

Tofu kebabs with miso pesto

1 red capsicum (pepper), cubed
12 button mushrooms, halved
6 pickling onions, quartered
3 zucchini (courgettes), cut into
   chunks
450 g (1 lb) firm tofu, cubed
125 ml (4 fl oz/½ cup) light
   olive oil
3 tablespoons light soy sauce
2 garlic cloves, crushed
2 teaspoons grated fresh ginger

Miso pesto
90 g (3¼ oz/½ cup) unsalted
   roasted peanuts
60 g (2¼ oz) coriander
   (cilantro) leaves
2 tablespoons white miso paste
2 garlic cloves
100 ml (3½ fl oz) olive oil

Soak 12 wooden skewers in water for 30 minutes. Thread the vegetables and tofu alternately onto the skewers, then place in a large non-metallic dish.

Mix together the olive oil, soy sauce, garlic and ginger, then pour half over the kebabs. Cover and leave to marinate for 1 hour.

To make the miso pesto, finely chop the peanuts, coriander leaves, miso paste and garlic in a food processor. Slowly add the olive oil while the machine is still running and blend to a smooth paste.

Cook the kebabs on a hot, lightly oiled barbecue grill or flat plate, turning and brushing with the remaining marinade, for 4–6 minutes, or until the edges are slightly brown. Serve with the miso pesto.

SERVES 4

Bruschetta with mushrooms

5 small field mushrooms, quartered

1 red onion, halved and thinly sliced

170 ml (5½ fl oz/⅔ cup) olive oil

3 garlic cloves, crushed

1½ tablespoons chopped oregano leaves

60 g (2½ oz/¼ cup) crème fraîche

1 teaspoon dijon mustard

1 loaf ciabatta bread

3 tablespoons olive oil, extra

1 garlic clove, extra, peeled and halved

small oregano leaves, to garnish

Put the mushrooms and onion in separate bowls and season each well. Whisk together the oil, garlic and oregano and pour two-thirds of the mixture over the mushrooms and the rest over the onion. Toss until well coated in the marinade, then cover and refrigerate for 30 minutes. Mix the crème fraîche and mustard together, then refrigerate until needed.

Heat a barbecue grill plate to medium direct heat. Cut the bread into twelve 1 cm (½ inch) thick slices and brush both sides of each slice with the extra oil. Toast the bread on the grill plate for 1–2 minutes on each side or until golden, then rub one side of each slice with the cut side of the garlic clove. Cook the onion on the flat plate for 2–3 minutes, or until golden. Cook the mushrooms on the flat plate for 2 minutes each side, then toss the onion and mushrooms together.

Arrange the mushrooms and onion on the garlic side of the bread slices and top with a teaspoon of mustard crème fraîche. Garnish with oregano leaves and season.

SERVES 6

Vegetable salad with balsamic dressing

4 baby eggplants (aubergine)
5 roma (plum) tomatoes
2 red capsicums (peppers)
1 green capsicum (pepper)
2 zucchini (courgettes)
100 ml (3½ fl oz) olive oil
12 bocconcini (fresh baby mozzarella cheese)
45 g (1½ oz/¼ cup) Ligurian olives
1 garlic clove, finely chopped
3 teaspoons baby capers
½ teaspoon sugar
2 tablespoons balsamic vinegar

Cut the eggplants and tomatoes in half lengthways. Cut the red and green capsicums in half lengthways, remove the seeds and membrane then cut each half into 3 pieces. Thinly slice the zucchini on the diagonal.

Preheat a barbecue grill plate. Add 1 tablespoon of oil and cook a quarter of the vegetables (cook the tomatoes cut-side down first) for about 2–3 minutes, or until marked and golden. Put in a bowl.

Cook the remaining vegetables in batches until tender, adding more oil as needed. Transfer to the bowl and add the bocconcini. Mix the olives, garlic, capers, sugar, vinegar and remaining oil (about 2 tablespoons). Pour over the salad and toss. Season with pepper.

SERVES 4–6

Chargrilled vegetables with basil aïoli

Basil aïoli
1 garlic clove
15 g (¼ oz) torn basil leaves
1 egg yolk
125 ml (4 fl oz/½ cup) olive oil
2 teaspoons lemon juice

2 large red capsicums (peppers), quartered, core and seeds removed
1 eggplant (aubergine), cut in 5 mm (¼ inch) thick rounds

1 orange sweet potato, peeled and cut on the diagonal into 5 mm (¼ inch) thick rounds
3 zucchini (courgettes), sliced lengthways into 5 mm (¼ inch) thick slices
2 red onions, cut into 1 cm (½ inch) thick rounds
4 tablespoons olive oil
1 loaf Turkish bread, split and cut into 4 equal pieces

To make the basil aïoli, put the garlic, basil and egg yolk in a food processor and blend until smooth. With the motor running, gradually add the oil in a thin stream. Stir in the lemon juice and season. Cover and refrigerate.

Preheat a barbecue grill plate to medium direct heat. Cook the capsicum, skin-side down, for 8–10 minutes or until the skin has softened and is blistering.

Meanwhile, brush the eggplant, sweet potato, zucchini and onion slices on both sides with olive oil and season. Cook the vegetables in batches on the middle of the chargrill for 5–8 minutes, or until cooked through but still firm. Grill the Turkish bread on both sides until it is lightly marked and toasted. Spread both cut sides of the bread with 1 tablespoon of basil aïoli and pile on some of the chargrilled vegetables. Top with the remaining toast and serve immediately.

SERVES 4

Stuffed eggplant

2 eggplants (aubergines)
2 tablespoons olive oil
1 onion, chopped
2 garlic cloves, crushed
4 tomatoes, roughly chopped
2 teaspoons tomato paste
   (concentrated purée)
2 tablespoons chopped dill

2 tablespoons chopped flat-leaf
   (Italian) parsley
2 tablespoons currants
2 tablespoons pine nuts
1 tablespoon red wine vinegar
150 g (5½ oz/1½ cups) finely
   grated kefalotyri cheese

Cut each eggplant in half lengthways and use a sharp knife to cut out the flesh, leaving a 5 mm (¼ inch) thick shell. Finely dice the flesh, toss it with 2 teaspoons of salt and drain in a colander over a bowl for 30 minutes. Squeeze out any excess moisture from the eggplant, rinse under cold water and drain on paper towels.

Heat 1 tablespoon oil in a frying pan over high heat. Add the diced eggplant and cook, stirring frequently, for 5 minutes, or until browned. Transfer to a bowl. Heat the remaining olive oil in the frying pan over medium heat, cook the onion and garlic for 2 minutes, then add the tomato, tomato paste, dill, parsley, currants, pine nuts and vinegar. Stir together and cook for 8–10 minutes, stirring occasionally. Add the tomato mixture to the eggplant with 100 g (3½ oz/1 cup) of the kefalotyri, season with black pepper and mix it together well.

Spoon the vegetable mixture into the eggplant shells and sprinkle with the remaining cheese.

Preheat a kettle or covered barbecue to medium indirect heat and put the eggplants in the middle of the barbecue. Cover and cook for 30 minutes, or until cooked through. Serve with a green salad.

SERVES 4

Mushroom and eggplant skewers

12 long rosemary sprigs
18 Swiss brown mushrooms,
  halved
1 small eggplant (aubergine),
  cubed
3 tablespoons olive oil
2 tablespoons balsamic vinegar
2 garlic cloves, crushed
1 teaspoon sugar

Tomato sauce
5 tomatoes
1 tablespoon olive oil
1 small onion, finely chopped
1 garlic clove, crushed
1 tablespoon tomato paste
  (concentrated purée)
2 teaspoons sugar
2 teaspoons balsamic vinegar
1 tablespoon chopped flat-leaf
  (Italian) parsley

Remove the leaves from the lower part of the rosemary sprigs. Reserve 1 tablespoon of the leaves. Put the mushrooms and eggplant in a large non-metallic bowl. Pour on the combined oil, vinegar, garlic and sugar and toss. Marinate for about 15 minutes.

To make the tomato sauce, score a cross in the base of each tomato. Put in a bowl of boiling water for 30 seconds, then plunge into cold water. Peel the skin away from the cross. Cut in half and scoop out the seeds with a teaspoon. Dice the flesh.

Heat the oil in a saucepan. Cook the onion and garlic over medium heat for 2–3 minutes, or until soft. Reduce the heat, add the tomato, tomato paste, sugar, vinegar and parsley and simmer for 10 minutes, or until thick.

Carefully thread alternating mushroom halves and eggplant cubes onto the rosemary sprigs. Cook on a hot, lightly oiled barbecue grill plate for 7–8 minutes, or until the eggplant is tender, turning occasionally. Serve with the sauce.

SERVES 4

Vegetarian skewers

5 thin zucchini (courgettes), cut into 2 cm (¾ inch) cubes
5 slender eggplants (aubergines), cut into 2 cm (¾ inch) cubes
12 button mushrooms, halved
2 red capsicums (peppers), cut into 2 cm (¾ inch) cubes
250 g (9 oz) kefalotyri cheese, cut into 2 cm (¾ inch) pieces

4 tablespoons lemon juice
2 garlic cloves, finely chopped
5 tablespoons finely chopped basil
145 ml (5 fl oz) extra virgin olive oil
couscous, to serve
lemon wedges, to serve

Using 12 metallic skewers, thread alternate pieces of vegetables and kefalotyri, starting and finishing with capsicum and using two pieces of kefalotyri per skewer. Put in a large non-metallic dish. Combine the lemon juice, garlic, 4 tablespoons of basil and 125 ml (4 fl oz/½ cup) of oil in a non-metallic bowl. Season. Pour two-thirds of the marinade over the skewers, reserving the remainder. Turn the skewers to coat evenly, cover with plastic wrap and marinate for at least 5 minutes.

Heat a barbecue flat plate to medium–high. Cook the skewers, brushing often with the leftover marinade, for 4–5 minutes each side, or until the vegetables are cooked and the cheese browns.

Drizzle the skewers with the reserved marinade. Serve immediately with lemon wedges and couscous, if desired.

SERVES 4

Vegetarian burgers with coriander garlic cream

250 g (9 oz/1 cup) red lentils
1 tablespoon oil
2 onions, sliced
1 tablespoon tandoori mix
 powder
425 g (15 oz) tinned chickpeas,
 drained
1 tablespoon grated fresh ginger
1 egg
3 tablespoons chopped flat-leaf
 (Italian) parsley
2 tablespoons chopped
 coriander (cilantro) leaves

180 g (6½ oz/2¼ cups) fresh
 breadcrumbs
plain (all-purpose) flour, to dust

Coriander garlic cream
125 g (4½ oz/½ cup) sour cream
125 ml (4 fl oz/½ cup) pouring
 (whipping) cream
1 garlic clove, crushed
2 tablespoons chopped
 coriander (cilantro) leaves
2 tablespoons chopped flat-leaf
 (Italian) parsley

Simmer the lentils in a saucepan of water for 8 minutes or until tender. Drain well. Heat the oil in a frying pan and cook the onion until tender. Add the tandoori mix and stir until fragrant.

Put the chickpeas, half the lentils, the ginger, egg and onion mixture in a food processor. Process for 20 seconds or until smooth. Transfer to a bowl. Stir in the remaining lentils, parsley, coriander and breadcrumbs.

Divide into 10 portions and shape into burgers. Toss in flour and place on a hot barbecue grill plate. Cook for 3–4 minutes each side or until browned.

To make the coriander garlic cream, mix together the sour cream, cream, garlic and herbs. Serve with the burgers.

MAKES 10 BURGERS

index

A

apple raita 113
Asian pork ribs 86
Asian-style seafood 148
asparagus with salsa 176
aubergine *see* egggplant

B

basil aïoli 187
beef
    beef kebabs with mint yoghurt dressing 14
    beef and mozzarella burgers with tomatoes 17
    beef satay skewers 10
    cheeseburger with capsicum salsa 18
    fillet steak with flavoured butters 22
    pepper steaks with horseradish sauce 33
    roast beef with barbecue sauce 38
    roast sirloin with mustard pepper crust 34
    rosemary and red wine steaks with vegetables 30
    sesame and ginger beef 29
    steak with balsamic onions 26
    steak sandwich with balsamic onions 13
    Thai beef skewers with peanut sauce 21
bruschetta with mushrooms 183

C

Cajun spiced chicken, blackened 105
capsicum salsa 18
cheeseburger with capsicum salsa 18
chermoula 135
chermoula prawns 151
chicken
    blackened Cajun spiced chicken 105
    chicken tikka with garlic naan and apple raita 113
    crispy chicken wings 114
    drumsticks in tomato and mango chutney 110
    five-spice roast chicken 122
    honey chicken wings 106
    honey mustard chicken 118
    Lebanese chicken 121
    lime and coriander chargrilled chicken 125
    Mediterranean chicken skewers 98
    Persian chicken skewers 109
    spicy buffalo wings with ranch dressing 101
    Thai spiced chicken with potato rosti 117
    yakitori chicken burgers 102
chickpeas, lamb pide with garlic and chickpea purée 50
chilli
    chilli pork ribs 81
    sweet chilli octopus 139
Chinese-style barbecue spare ribs 73
coriander prawns 131
corn in the husk 175
crab with Singapore-style pepper sauce 163

D

dill mayonnaise 156
drumsticks in tomato and mango chutney 110

E

eggplant
    eggplant with lemon pesto 179
    mushroom and eggplant skewers 191
    stuffed eggplant 188

F

fennel and pork sausages with onion relish 82
fish tikka 144
five-spice roast chicken 122

G

garlic and mint lamb
skewers with yoghurt
sauce 42
garlic naan 113
ginger–orange pork 89

H

herbed lamb burgers 46
hoisin lamb with charred
spring onion 58
honey chicken wings 106
honey and lime prawn
kebabs with salsa 136
honey mustard chicken
118
honey roasted pork fillet
94

K

king prawns with dill
mayonnaise 156

L

lamb
garlic and mint lamb
skewers with yoghurt
sauce 42
herbed lamb burgers 46
hoisin lamb with charred
spring onion 58
lamb burger 54
lamb chops with citrus
pockets 61
lamb cutlets with mint
gremolata 61
lamb kebabs 45
lamb kofta 49
lamb pide with garlic and
chickpea purée 50
lamb souvlaki roll 57
marinated lamb 65

paprika lamb kebabs
with skordalia 53
roast lamb 66
Lebanese chicken 121
lemon and herb yoghurt
128
lemon and sage veal chops
with rocket 25
lime and coriander
chargrilled chicken 125
lobster with burnt butter
sauce and grilled lemon
160

M

Malaysian barbecued
seafood 159
Mediterranean chicken
skewers 98
miso pesto 180
mushrooms
bruschetta with
mushrooms 183
mushroom and eggplant
skewers 191

O

octopus
chargrilled baby octopus
147
sweet chilli octopus 139
onion relish 82

P

paprika lamb kebabs with
skordalia 53
pepper steaks with
horseradish sauce 33
Persian chicken skewers
109
picada dressing 152
piri piri prawns 143

pork
Asian pork ribs 86
chilli pork ribs 81
Chinese-style barbecue
spare ribs 73
fennel and pork sausages
with onion relish 82
ginger–orange pork 89
honey roasted pork fillet
94
pork with apple and
onion wedges 93
pork loin with apple
glaze and wedges 85
pork sausage burgers
with mustard cream 77
pork skewers in green
ginger wine and soy 70
roast rack of pork with
chunky apple sauce
90
spice-rubbed pork
kebabs with garlic
sauce 74
sweet and sour pork
kebabs 78
potatoes
baby potatoes 172
potato rosti 117
prawns
chermoula prawns 151
coriander prawns 131
honey and lime prawn
kebabs with salsa 136
king prawns with dill
mayonnaise 156
piri piri prawns 143

R

ranch dressing 101
red mullet with herb sauce
168

rosemary and red wine
  steaks with vegetables
  30

S
salmon cutlets with sweet
  cucumber dressing 164
scallop and fish rosemary
  skewers 140
seafood
  Asian-style seafood 148
  chargrilled baby octopus
    147
  chermoula prawns 151
  coriander prawns 131
  crab with Singapore-style
    pepper sauce 163
  fish tikka 144
  honey and lime prawn
    kebabs with salsa 136
  king prawns with dill
    mayonnaise 156
  lobster with burnt butter
    sauce and grilled lemon
    160
  Malaysian barbecued
    seafood 159
  piri piri prawns 143
  red mullet with herb
    sauce 168
  salmon cutlets with
    sweet cucumber
    dressing 164
  scallop and fish rosemary
    skewers 140
  squid with picada
    dressing 152
  sweet chilli octopus 139
  swordfish with anchovy
    and caper sauce 167
  swordfish shish kebabs
    with herb yoghurt 128

swordfish with tomato
  butter 155
tuna burgers with herbed
  mayonnaise 132
tuna skewers with
  Moroccan spices 135
sesame and ginger beef
  29
skewers
  beef kebabs with mint
    yoghurt dressing 14
  beef satay skewers 10
  fish tikka 144
  garlic and mint lamb
    skewers with yoghurt
    sauce 42
  honey and lime prawn
    kebabs with salsa 136
  lamb kebabs 45
  Mediterranean chicken
    skewers 98
  mushroom and eggplant
    skewers 191
  paprika lamb kebabs
    with skordalia 53
  Persian chicken skewers
    109
  pork skewers in green
    ginger wine and soy 70
  scallop and fish rosemary
    skewers 140
  spice-rubbed pork
    kebabs with garlic
    sauce 74
  sweet and sour pork
    kebabs 78
  swordfish shish kebabs
    with herb yoghurt 128
  Thai beef skewers with
    peanut sauce 21
  tofu kebabs with miso
    pesto 180

tuna skewers with
  Moroccan spices 135
vegetarian skewers 192
spice-rubbed pork kebabs
  with garlic sauce 74
spicy buffalo wings with
  ranch dressing 101
squid with picada dressing
  152
steak
  fillet steak with flavoured
    butters 22
  pepper steaks with
    horseradish sauce 33
  rosemary and red wine
    steaks with vegetables
    30
  steak with balsamic
    onions 26
  steak sandwich with
    balsamic onions 13
sweet and sour pork
  kebabs 78
swordfish with anchovy
  and caper sauce 167
swordfish shish kebabs
  with herb yoghurt 128
swordfish with tomato
  butter 155

T
Thai beef skewers with
  peanut sauce 21
Thai spiced chicken with
  potato rosti 117
tofu kebabs with miso
  pesto 180
tomato sauce 191
tuna burgers with herbed
  mayonnaise 132
tuna skewers with
  Moroccan spices 135

V

veal
  lemon and sage veal
    chops with rocket 25
  veal steaks with caper
    butter 37
vegetables
  asparagus with salsa
    176
  baby potatoes 172
  bruschetta with
    mushrooms 183
  chargrilled vegetables
    with basil aïoli 187
  corn in the husk 175
  eggplant with lemon
    pesto 179
  mushroom and eggplant
    skewers 191
  stuffed eggplant 188
  vegetable salad with
    balsamic dressing 184
vegetarian burgers with
    coriander garlic cream
    195
vegetarian skewers 192

Y

yakitori chicken burgers
    102

First published in 2008 by Murdoch Books Pty Limited

Murdoch Books Australia
Pier 8/9, 23 Hickson Road
Millers Point NSW 2000
Phone: +61 (0) 2 8220 2000
Fax: +61 (0) 2 8220 2558
www.murdochbooks.com.au

Murdoch Books UK Limited
Erico House, 6th Floor
93–99 Upper Richmond Road,
Putney, London SW15 2TG
Phone: +44 (0) 20 8785 5995
Fax: +44 (0) 20 8785 5985
www.murdochbooks.co.uk

Chief Executive: Juliet Rogers
Publishing Director: Kay Scarlett

Design Manager: Vivien Valk
Project manager and editor: Gordana Trifunovic
Design concept: Alex Frampton
Designer: Susanne Geppert
Production: Nikla Martin
Introduction text: Leanne Kitchen
Cover photography: Tanya Zouev
Styling: Stephanie Souvlis
Recipes developed by the Murdoch Books Test Kitchen

Printed by Sing Cheong Printing Co. Ltd in 2008. PRINTED IN HONG KONG.
Reprinted 2008.

ISBN 978 1 74196 115 7 (pbk.).
A catalogue record for this book is available from the British Library.

IMPORTANT: Those who might be at risk from the effects of salmonella poisoning (the
elderly, pregnant women, young children and those suffering from immune deficiency
diseases) should consult their doctor with any concerns about eating raw eggs.

CONVERSION GUIDE: You may find cooking times vary depending on the oven you are
using. For fan-forced ovens, as a general rule, set the oven temperature to 20°C (35°F)
lower than indicated in the recipe.